tall buildings
a strategic design guide

Edited by
Ziona Strelitz

british council for
offices

RIBA Publishing

© BCO, 2005
Published by RIBA Publishing, 15 Bonhill Street, London EC2P 2EA

ISBN 1 85946 168 9

Stock Code: 39213

The right of the named contributors to be identified as the authors of their respective sections
has been asserted in accordance with the Copyright, Design and Patents Act 1988.

British Library Cataloguing in Publications Data
A catalogue record for this book is available from the British Library.

Editor: Ziona Strelitz
Publisher: Steven Cross
Commissioning Editor: Matthew Thompson
Project Editor: Anna Walters
Designed by: Kneath Associates
Printed in the United Kingdom by CPI Bath

Cover illustration taken from fig on p70–1 © KPF

tall buildings
a strategic design guide

published by

The British Council for Offices and RIBA Publishing

contributing firms

Arup

Davis Langdon

Kohn Pedersen Fox Associates (International) PA

Lerch Bates & Associates

ZZA

edited by Ziona Strelitz

BCO Tall Buildings Working Party:

Alastair Collins (Chairman) Davis Langdon

Clive Arding and Peter Damesick CB Richard Ellis

Richard Kauntze and Ian Selby BCO

Gerald Kaye Helical Bar

Michael Lowndes TP Bennett

Lee Polisano and Fred Pilbrow Kohn Pedersen Fox

Gerald Powell Baynard Developments

Ziona Strelitz ZZA

Christopher Strickland Greycoat

Faith Wainwright Arup

David Watkins Linklaters

Dedicated to the memory of Tony Fitzpatrick of Arup, 1951-2003, distinguished engineer and enthusiastic member of the BCO Tall Buildings Working Party

RIBA ⅲ Publishing

contents

foreword:

ALASTAIR COLLINS,
CHAIR, BCO
TALL BUILDINGS GROUP

The skylines of many world cities – and of those cities contending for such recognition – are defined and punctuated by tall buildings.

The drivers for such dominant skylines range from land scarcity and social needs; high real estate values, commercial opportunity and corporate demand, through to metropolitan signposting – the skyline of San Gimignano in the fourteenth century being the equivalent of Europe's Manhattan.

Accepting the complexity of the local, national and international agendas for tall buildings, the work which follows emphasises the need for contextual relevance and high quality of design – of urban infrastructure, architecture, and structural, mechanical, electrical, life safety and transportation engineering – as fundamental to the commercial viability and sustainability of tall buildings, individually and collectively, in an urban habitat.

This distinctive work complements the three previous publications by the BCO Tall Buildings Working Group:

↘ Guidance on Planning (offering guidelines for a successful planning application)

↘ The Economic Realities (of developing, owning or occupying a tall building)

↘ Giving Occupiers a Voice (a survey of owners and occupiers of tall buildings, presenting their views)

This Strategic Guide provides a valuable reference for anyone contemplating a tall building or seeking confirmation of the essential criteria for sustainable design.

technical, cultural and policy context:

⬎ Aim: Target audience

ZIONA STRELITZ ZZA

This guide overviews the technical perspectives relevant to tall buildings. It is aimed at clients who are considering commissioning tall buildings, statutory authorities, other agencies and members of the public who seek to understand the distinct issues relating to these constructions.

The issues concern urban design, architecture, engineering, life safety, construction and market economics and building occupancy. The inputs have been provided by practitioners with specialist knowledge in the respective fields. This publication is not an in-depth guide to producing a tall building, but rather a 'road map' of key aspects to consider in generating, understanding and evaluating tall building proposals.

Together with *Tall Buildings in London: Guidance on Planning*, Linklaters (2002), *Tall Buildings in London: The Economic Reality*, Insignia Richard Ellis (2002) and *Tall Buildings in London: Giving Occupiers a Voice*, ZZA (2002), this guide completes the BCO's 'quartet' of publications on tall buildings.

The BCO offers comprehensive design guidance on office buildings of conventional height in its *Best Practice in the Specification for Offices 2005*. In contrast, the guidance presented here is specific to tall buildings, and does not overlap with information provided in the BCO Specification.

Geographical focus

The geographical frame for this work is primarily the UK, with a focus on London, where attention to high buildings has gathered steam in recent years. This is evident in trends on the supply side and the regulatory context. These include:

⬎ The strategic stance in favour of high buildings by the Greater London Authority – notably in *The London Plan: The Mayor's Spatial Development Strategy*.

⬎ An increase in the number of proposals to construct tall buildings.

⬎ The granting of planning consent to new tall building proposals such as the Heron and Minerva Towers and 122 Leadenhall Street in the City of London, London Bridge Tower in Southwark and Columbus Tower in Tower Hamlets.

← Heron Tower, 110 Bishopsgate, view from Threadneedle Street. The proposals by KPF which received planning consent in 2002, following a public inquiry, are for one of a new generation of tall buildings proposed for the City of London.
© Hayes Davidson/KPF

◥ The recent completion of numerous new tall buildings in a number of London locations – Paddington, the City and Canary Wharf.

◥ The successful refurbishment of previous generations of tall buildings, such as Tower 42 and Citipoint.

London is not the only UK location where tall buildings are topical. There has been significant wider interest in existing and new tall buildings – in Birmingham, Liverpool, Manchester and Brighton by way of example. Nevertheless, the London context reflects the foci of this guide, which describes the features that distinguish a tall building from buildings of conventional height, in technical, functional and aesthetic as well as in planning terms. However, the reference to London is illustrative; the points it evidences relate to other settings as well.

Evolution in policy

Associated with the groundswell of interest in tall buildings has been a change in the policy context, with new support for tall buildings after a hiatus of over two decades. These include:

Metropolitan and Local Government

◥ The re-establishment of a strategic planning authority for London in 2000. The Greater London Authority (GLA), created by the Greater London Authority Act of 1999, assumed its main responsibilities in July the following year. It has furthered the interest in tall buildings taken by its predecessor, the London Planning Advisory Committee (LPAC) in LPAC's *Strategic Planning Advice on High Buildings and Strategic Views in London* (1999). The GLA argues that London must cater for its projected population growth to 8.1 million people by 2016, with 636,000 new jobs being created over this period, in order to maintain its status as a global city. The *London Plan*, published in February 2004, seeks to accommodate this growth without sacrificing London's open spaces and green belt. Significantly for this objective, tall buildings are identified as a mechanism to facilitate increased densities, at locations with good public transport.

◥ All London local authorities are now required to bring their local plans into broad compliance with the Mayor's London Plan.

◥ Some London local authorities, e.g. the Corporation of London and the London Boroughs of Southwark, Croydon and Hackney, have themselves been supportive of tall buildings, arguing that they promote economic development.

Recent tall buildings and tall building proposals

↓ Swiss Re, 30 St Mary Axe, City of London, designed by Foster and Partners, and completed in 2004.
© Nigel Young/Foster and Partners

◥ London Bridge Tower, Southwark, designed by Renzo Piano Building Workshop, with planning consent granted in November 2003 following a public inquiry.
© Hays Davidson/John Mclean

◥◥ Minerva Building, City of London, designed by Grimshaw and Partners, with planning consent granted in January 2004.
© Smoothe Ltd.

Statutory and non-statutory consultees

⬊ The replacement of the Royal Fine Art Commission (RFAC) by the Commission for Architecture and the Built Environment (CABE) in 1999 has resulted in championship for quality architecture and urban design. CABE is a non-statutory planning consultee. CABE's joint publication with English Heritage, *Guidance on Tall Buildings* (2003), has contributed to the policy context in which tall building proposals are assessed. As a statutory consultee, English Heritage has adopted a thoughtful view. Whilst objecting to tall building proposals on sites which it deems inappropriate, it has supported other proposals for tall buildings (e.g. 30 St Mary Axe and 122 Leadenhall Street), recognising that they can have architectural, urban and economic merit.

↓ Brunswick Quay, Liverpool, designed by Ian Simpson Architects, submitted for planning in 2004.
© Smoothe Ltd

→ 122 Leadenhall Street, City of London, designed by Richard Rogers Partnership, with planning consent granted in 2004.
© Richard Rogers Partnership/CityScape

Central Government

↘ To the extent that tall buildings can provide for increased densities (meeting the 'Urban Renaissance' agenda) and reduced use of private cars for travel to work (meeting 'Kyoto objectives'), they accord with the Government's focus on sustainable development.

Critics have argued that tall buildings are not the only means to increase urban density. Although the latter view was shared by the Transport, Local Government and Regional Affairs Select Committee's report on tall buildings (2002), the government has taken a more positive approach. It observes that "high rise buildings generally require smaller sites than low rise buildings with big floorplates offering an equivalent amount of space". It therefore endorses the CABE/English Heritage guidance, encouraging local authorities to prepare policies in relation to tall buildings policies and to designate areas in their local plans where tall buildings would, and would not, be deemed appropriate.

Whilst tall buildings have an inherent requirement for energy use on vertical travel and through their relatively high ratio of external façade to floor area, their actual environmental performance depends on a variety of factors associated with their location, design and specification. Recent proposals have harnessed advanced modelling and analysis tools to integrate the performance of the building's orientation, envelope, services and management, as a basis for achieving ambitious energy targets.

↘ The Government's support for tall buildings is reflected in the Deputy Prime Minister's endorsement of planning consent for both the Heron Tower and London Bridge Tower, in line with the recommendations of the respective planning inquiries for each of these proposals.

↑ Grand Union Building, Paddington, Westminster, designed by Richard Rogers Partnership, with planning consent granted in January 2003.
© Richard Rogers Partnership/Hayes Davidson

→ Beetham Tower Manchester, designed by Ian Simpson Architects, under construction in 2005.
© www.uniform.net

→→ New London Bridge House, Southwark (right of London Bridge Tower), design proposal by KPF in 2004.
© GMJ

How tall?

The guide focuses on tall buildings in the range of 20–60 storeys. This is a pragmatic range for a UK review, as the lower end is the height at which tall buildings start to become technically distinct, whilst the upper end relates to existing UK buildings and recent proposals for new tall buildings. Seen in an international context, however, UK building heights are modest, and might be called 'mid-height' rather than tall.

→   Existing and proposed tall buildings in the UK are modest in scale compared to international examples.
© KPF

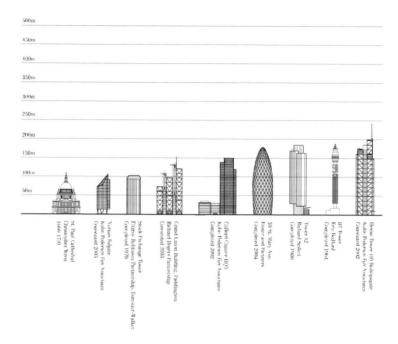

↓   London skyline from St Paul's Gallery.
© Hayes Davidson/KPF

↘   New York City skyline.
© KPF

↘↘   Hong Kong skyline.
© Gavin Hellier/Getty Images

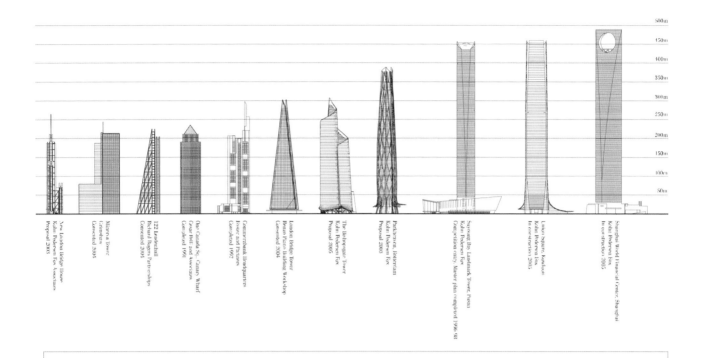

500m
450m
400m
350m
300m
250m
200m
150m
100m
50m

New London Bridge House
Kohn Pedersen Fox Associates
Proposal 2005

Minerva Tower
Grimshaw
Consented 2005

122 Leadenhall
Richard Rogers Partnerships
Consented 2005

One Canada Sq., Canary Wharf
Cesar Pelli and Associates
Completed 1991

Commerzbank Headquarters
Foster and Partners
Completed 1997

London Bridge Tower
Renzo Piano Building Workshop
Consented 2004

The Bishopsgate Tower
Kohn Pedersen Fox
Proposal 2005

Parkhaven, Rotterdam
Kohn Pedersen Fox
Proposal 2005

Suyoung Bay Landmark Tower, Pusan
Kohn Pedersen Fox
Competition entry. Master plan completed 1996-98

Union Square, Kowloon
Kohn Pedersen Fox
In construction 2005

Shanghai World Financial Centre, Shanghai
Kohn Pedersen Fox
In construction 2005

↘ Seen in an international context, UK building heights are modest, and might be called 'mid-height' rather than tall.

> ↘ A tall building is not a low building that is simply extruded vertically, but one that is differently designed.

What defines a tall building?
Scale in local context

A plausible definition of a tall building in town planning terms may be one that rises above the prevailing skyline. Whilst this guide accepts that the relation of vertical scale to its context is key for urban design, the definition used here rests on tall buildings' technical and design differentiation, as well as on their contextual distinction. Put another way, a tall building is not a low building that is simply extruded vertically, but one that is differently designed.

Structure, services, life safety and cost

The focus adopted here:

↘ Indicates the thresholds at which tall buildings become technically distinct.

↘ Outlines the associated features of this distinction associated with building structure, services, life safety and cost.

A substantive differentiator between a tall building and one of more conventional height includes the former's vertical circulation relative to internal area, with the resultant economic implications for the efficiency of both the building's enclosed space and its construction. The factors that influence these efficiencies change as a conventional building becomes a tall building at the height of around 20 storeys. They vary again as the building increases in height, although the relationship is not even. Rather, it is defined by step-changes in the inter-relationships of the key specification elements, most especially by the size of the usable floor plate relative to core area.

Tall buildings are technically distinct from buildings of conventional height and require specialist design for their structure, envelope, vertical transportation, other services and life safety systems. Over thirty consultant disciplines provided input into the Heron Plaza proposals.

← Heron Plaza, Bishopsgate, London, designed by KPF, consented in 2004.
© GMJ

Cultural perspective
Cultural impacts

Whilst the focus adopted here is tall buildings' technical distinction, their cultural influences have other impacts. This is evident in the responses which tall buildings evoke. Whilst proposals for tall buildings typically elicit excitement in their promise or concern over their alteration to the status quo, once built, the norms and connotations surrounding them tend to adopt a new equilibrium.

Lesson of hindsight

This is illustrated by an historical perspective. When buildings like Liverpool's 'Three Graces' were constructed to accommodate the city's prospering insurance industry in the early twentieth century, the gap between prevailing building heights and the heights established by these new waterfront buildings was significant. The 'Three Graces' provide an important cultural reference, as their design which was radical when first constructed now strikes an historicist chord. This has been illustrated by the recent proposal for a 'Fourth Grace'. Siting this new building alongside the three earlier towers would have inevitable implications for changing what has now become a heritage view, centred on Liverpool's then radical 20th century towers, which are now perceived as traditional.

Style and height

Key to the impact of the 'Fourth Grace' is its introduction of stylistic difference, rather than a difference in height per se. The proposed building's height is relevant due to its relative visibility as a canvas that manifests change. Equally, the height of the original three towers is relevant to those buildings' visibility. The cultural impact of added height promotes tall buildings as cultural icons.

↗   Proposal for a 'Fourth Grace' in Liverpool, by Alsop & Partners.
     © Alsop & Partners

→   Proposal for a 'Fourth Grace' in Liverpool, by Richard Rogers Partnership.
     © Richard Rogers Partnership/Melon Studio

Buildings inside and out

Cultural modes influence the internal design of tall buildings. Evolving concepts of what constitutes effective internal space are influencing tall building design in the UK. A combined focus on individuals' aspirations for natural daylight, and corporate objectives for floor plates that are well suited to accommodating teams, has resulted in tall buildings which cater for both these expectations. A building such as that commissioned by Swiss Re at 30 St Mary Axe reflects this cultural blend of corporate and individual interests.

International comparators

A design like that for Swiss Re is unlikely to have found a footing in the USA, where a less assertive agenda on internal spatial quality for individuals – as well as factors such as the availability of larger, more regular building plots – typically result in tall buildings with larger floor plates. Floor plates are less diverse in North America, where core to wall depths of 42' to 60' are standard. With the added floor space for their height that this involves, such buildings are economically more productive for their developers. However, in terms of the reduced level of natural lighting to their interior space, and their more limited views to the exterior, such buildings may not meet prevailing cultural preferences in the UK. The less constrained sites available in a peripheral UK location like Canary Wharf allow for tall buildings on the North American model. However, these buildings' deeper floor plates – relative to those found in the City of London – are at the shallower end of the dimensions common in North America.

UK design individuality

Individuality in the outward appearance of commercial buildings is embedded in UK cultural expectations. This reflects on the buildings' response to their respective sites, their interface with their context, and a preference for individualism in external expression on the part of local authorities, developers, architects and occupiers. Canary Wharf resembles a North American model also in this respect, with the location having a distinct aesthetic deriving from

Citigroup, Canary Wharf, designed by Foster and Partners.
↑ © Nigel Young/Foster and Partners
→ © Richard Davies

30 St Mary Axe, designed by Foster and Partners.
↖ © Nigel Young/Foster and Partners
← © Nigel Young/Foster and Partners

considerable stylistic synergy between the individual buildings.

The cost to produce bespoke or 'one-off' buildings is higher than the cost to procure buildings where design replication is more feasible and more accepted, and where individualism in design expression is not a norm. In settings such as Hong Kong, the focus on buildings' external individuality is also strong. Whilst this focus on external image helps to create value for buildings and localities in the Hong Kong setting, the interiors of these buildings tend not to reflect the spatial quality favoured by UK culture, despite notable exceptions such as the HSBC building designed by Foster and Partners.

UK building quality

UK tall building design is therefore distinguished on the international stage by its more individualistic architectural approach, externally as well as internally. These current cultural influences are resulting in buildings of consistently better quality. Although meeting these preferences results in outcomes which are comparatively costly, UK culture values building quality. The interest in quality is accentuated for new buildings of significant vertical scale. This has been demonstrated by the scrutiny applied at recent public inquiries to proposed tall buildings, on those aspects which impinge on both building and environmental quality.

↘ UK culture values building quality. The interest in quality is accentuated for new buildings of significant vertical scale.

London's circumstance
Urban ecology

London is a city with multiple centres. Its significant international position is achieved by its status as a premier capital city integrated into the global economy. These two distinct circumstances form a particular backdrop for tall building proposals.

↓   London has long been characterised as a polycentric city whose growth has subsumed a number of formerly independent centres. This history has enriched the built fabric of the city and allowed a variety of building types to respond to distinct needs. A number of tall building clusters across the capital, shown below, reflect recent additions to this historic process. A future cluster is proposed at Stratford to the east and another potential cluster at Elephant and Castle to the south.
© KPF

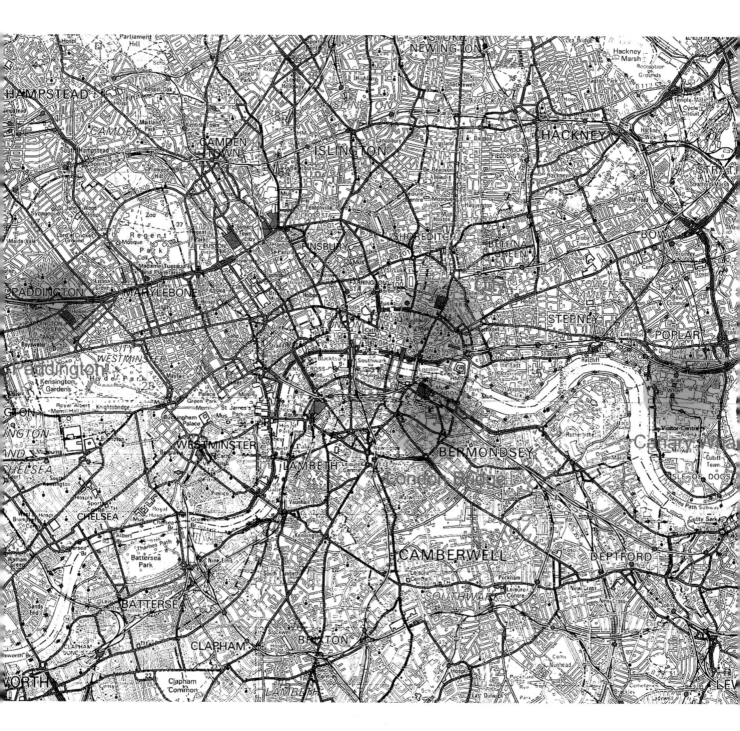

↓   The Canary Wharf cluster, to the right of the map opposite, is now a major centre for London's financial services.
© Canary Wharf Group plc

Economic and cultural aspirations

The city's economic ambitions and planning objectives seek to maintain and further London's position as a global economic centre. Tall buildings have two roles in this. They are seen as a symbol of progressive economic activity and prosperity, whilst functionally they offer appropriate accommodation to house the international businesses for which cities compete. At the same time, the heritage value of London's cityscape is recognised. People want the best of both the old and the new, and this balance is sought by people in international businesses operating in London, as it is by Londoners and their professional planners.

The recent proposals for quality tall buildings in concentrated 'clusters' on public transport nodes have resulted from a combination of conditions. Key is London's economic vigour, combined with a sense of patronage that is characteristic of an historic mercantile city. Second are the city's planning policies, which build on existing physical and economic clusters and public transport nodes.

→   The north east City cluster showing the consented
     Heron Tower and the completed Swiss Re building at
     30 St Mary Axe.
     © Hayes Davidson/KPF

↓   The north east City cluster (in the image left), and
     the London Bridge cluster (in the image right)
     including the proposed London Bridge Tower and
     New London Bridge House, planned to support the
     regeneration of Southwark.
     © GMJ

the occupants' perspective:

ZIONA STRELITZ ZZA

↘ **Why occupy tall buildings?** Tall office buildings provide for many objectives that occupiers have for their space. The relevance of these buildings is demonstrated by their occupancy levels. In both tight market conditions and periods of increased availability, space in tall buildings has been in demand. The space higher up in tall buildings may be especially favoured, commanding relative premiums.

Location

Where tall buildings are situated on a public transport node, they can offer good, environmentally friendly access to large numbers of staff. This is efficient for the occupier organisation and its staff, and in meeting evolving policy that favours environmentally sustainable travel to work. With increasing attention to corporate social responsibility as an aspect of governance, environmental responsibility in respect of travel to work is growing in importance.

The clustering of tall buildings in given locations affords scope for businesses in related sectors to co-locate. Locational clustering supports economic clustering, creating parts of the city with a critical mass of related activities, such as insurance brokerage, foreign banking and legal activity. This facilitates the development of local marketplaces for given sectors, with enhanced economic value.

← Interior view of an office 'village' at Heron Tower, 110 Bishopsgate, designed by KPF, showing the design's response to demands for higher environmental quality in the workplace. The triple-height north-facing atria provide for good daylighting and facilitate communication between individual floors.
© GMJ

Co-location

A key benefit which tall buildings offer is the opportunity to consolidate a large organisation, or part of it, within one envelope. In a city like London, where many building footprints are determined by historic street patterns, the scope for large amounts of space in buildings of lower height is inevitably limited. Even where large sites can be assembled, the impact of the resultant 'groundscrapers' can be out of scale with the established urban grain. Such buildings frustrate the physical and visual permeability considered key to good urban design.

The economic objective of large organisations occupying the same building to facilitate internal communication does not necessarily require large floor plates. It can be achieved on multiple floors of a tall building that has smaller floors, benefiting the occupier by providing a large amount of space within one envelope. It also offers urban advantages, allowing for more physical and visual permeability than large low buildings typically permit. Tall buildings can therefore meet businesses' economic objectives by offering them scope to consolidate within a single building, whilst contributing to good urban design.

↓   Lloyds of London headquarters, designed by Richard Rogers Partnership, completed in 1986, enabling Lloyds to sublet a proportion of the building to other insurance companies seeking to be located close to the main insurance trading floor.
© Richard Rogers Partnership

→   Arcaid/Photographer: Richard Bryant

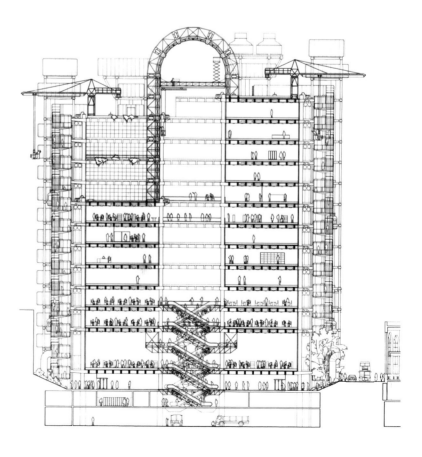

Identity

A tall building provides an easily identifiable address. The signature of height is not only an asset for a sole occupier. Multi-let tall buildings, like Tower 42 in the City and 1 Canada Square in Canary Wharf, provide a positive identity for smaller occupiers who share tenancy at these addresses. Older tall buildings like Millbank Tower and Centrepoint have also been successful in providing the advantage of address for a range of tenants.

Aspect and light

People usually prefer workspace with both an external view and natural light. Tall buildings in the UK, often with floor plates of relatively shallow depth, have more scope to provide for these benefits than low buildings with large floor plates.

↗   10 Upper Bank Street, Canary Wharf, designed by KPF, and completed in 2004, affords the occupier, Clifford Chance, appropriate floor plate sizes, excellent daylight and external aspect from the interior, as well as a high quality building image.
© H.G. Esch

→   © www.foliophotography.co.uk

Amenity and support

Contemporary organisations seek a range of internal facilities and settings in addition to the large areas of desks and classic meeting rooms that have long constituted the bulk of office space. These complementary facilities include cafés and other informal meeting venues to support business operations, as well as amenities such as gyms to support staff's lifestyle needs. Tall buildings, especially those with large floor plates, have the scale to accommodate these facilities. Siting these uses on discrete floors can also create distinct 'addresses' inside a tall building, enriching the building's sense of place internally.

The scale of 10 Upper Bank Street enables Clifford Chance to offer its staff a high level of amenity within the building. The swimming pool, gym and staff restaurant benefit from good daylight and fine external views, as does the workspace.

↖   © H.G Esch
←   © H.G Esch
↓   © Clifford Chance

Security

The concern for building security in the UK, which was already strong following political events of the 1980s, intensified in 2001 after 11 September 2001. The iconic nature of tall buildings and the physical concentration of value that they represent on one site may dispose them as a target for terrorism. However, tall buildings can facilitate effective security operations. Their more compact footprints and concentrated vertical circulation cores make for fewer points that require surveillance and access control, although these may be relatively easy to disable in the event of an attack.

Productivity

Tall buildings serve an economic role in meeting business objectives. They therefore facilitate productive activity in their internal space. To the extent that they form local clusters, they also promote economic synergy in their localities. Further, the provision of rental accommodation in tall buildings contributes to useful premises choice for occupiers, increasing organisations' scope to meet their spatial requirements.

In these respects, and in meeting those occupiers' needs that tall buildings uniquely serve, these structures promote productivity for their occupiers and competitive advantage for their localities. This is relevant to districts, cities and national economies.

User comfort

Occupiers seeking the above benefits would not wish to detract from the values that such accommodation offers with conditions that irritate people working in or visiting their buildings. Comfort matters! Chapter 4 identifies how design can address the distinct challenges to comfort posed by tall buildings with positive effect. The discussion covers vertical circulation, structural stability and wind-induced oscillation, internal environmental quality and life safety.

HSBC, Canary Wharf, designed by Foster and Partners, completed in 2002 .
↑   © Nigel Young/Foster and Partners
→   Typical floor plan.
© Foster and Partners

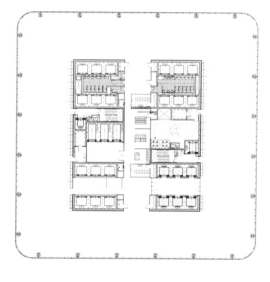

New building to accommodate co-
location by Barclays at Canary
Wharf, designed by HOK
Architects, completed in 2004.
© www.foliophotography.co.uk
→ Typical floor plan, showing fit-out
plan, by Pringle Brandon
Architects.
© Pringle Brandon

Contemporary
work modes

The attraction of 'big space'

A major differentiator between types of
tall building is size of the floor plate.
Many large floors – of 2-3,000 m² each –
provide a big quantum of space within a
single building – say 80-100,000 m²
overall. Such buildings suit organisations
in a number of different business
sectors – typically financial and
professional services. Such occupiers
select tall buildings in order to
accommodate all or many parts of their
organisation together in one building.

Value of communication

The business benefit that this 'co-
location' achieves is easier internal
communication, with scope to share
market knowledge between individuals
and different parts of the business,
exchange ideas, transfer knowledge,
pass on referrals, cross-sell services and
reinforce the occupier's organisational
culture. The latter is especially relevant
where a new ethos needs to be forged
from the respective cultures and
identities of previously separate
organisations, now amalgamated by
merger or acquisition.

Work and living patterns

A significant secondary benefit of a large
amount of space is scope to
accommodate support facilities such as
auditoria, client entertaining venues,
sports and other amenities within one
building. Where work practices are
strongly customer-focused, staff
frequently stay at the workplace for long
periods. A building's capacity to meet the
needs of busy staff within the building,
in the evening and on weekends, is
beneficial. Large floor plate buildings
have particular scope to incorporate
such provision.

Big and bigger

Tall buildings with large floor plates are
suited to a wide range of general office
functions. The scope to place these floor
plates on a building base with a larger
footprint – of 5,000-7,500m² – enables
an even wider range of functions. Trading
operations needing 700-900 staff per
floor are a case in point.

Smaller tall buildings

Tall buildings with smaller floor plates have a distinct appeal. They suit organisations that have far fewer people to accommodate within one building. They may also suit organisations that do not need an entire building for themselves.

One benefit that this provides for smaller organisations is identity. This derives from a tall building's landmark quality. Another benefit is shared facilities and services. The amount of space and related service charge that even a smaller tall building can support may allow for facilities such as retail outlets or concierge services within the building. The ability to have these benefits in dense urban areas such as the City of London, where small building footprints would preclude these complementary facilities in buildings of conventional height, is a particular advantage.

Older tall buildings

Any city should consider the risk of building redundancy, particularly for more extreme buildings types that may be less adaptable to change and harder to demolish. The research finding that older tall buildings are actively occupied and used underscores the relevance of tall buildings (*Tall Office Buildings in London: Giving Occupiers a Voice, ZZA, BCO 2002*). The factors that make older tall buildings attractive to occupiers include good daylight inside, good views out, and height. Together these confer the benefits of internal spatial building identity and quality which appeal to staff.

Tenant range

A varied tall building stock supports a diverse tenant profile. Occupiers are influenced by:

- Floor plate size
- The amount of space in the building overall
- The sectoral focus in the locality
- Sole occupancy and multi-let opportunities
- The quality and nature of shared services which the building can support

- Its period of construction
- Rent levels and terms
- Service charges.

London's tall building occupiers include major international firms, government and other public sector organisations and small niche businesses. This tenant profile reflects on the supportive role of tall buildings and a diverse tall building stock in promoting a city's economic life.

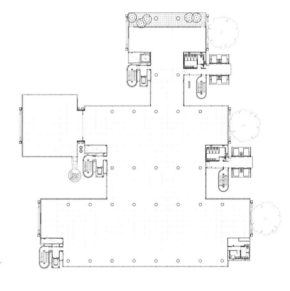

Multi-tenanted tall space at 88 Wood Street, London, designed by Richard Rogers Partnership, and completed in 1999.
➔➔ © Richard Rogers Partnership Photographer: Katsuisha Kida.

Typical floor plan.
➔ © Richard Rogers Partnership/Melon Studio

Successfully refurbished older tall buildings:

Millbank Tower, Millbank, London.
↓ © Justin Piperger

Centrepoint, Tottenham Court Road, London.
↘ © Justin Piperger

design aims:
urban focus

↘Tall buildings are highly visible. Designed well, and in the right locations, they can make a powerful contribution to the quality and vitality of their setting. They can also contribute to sustainable urban development. However, poorly designed, or in the wrong location, they can detract from their context. Proposals for new tall buildings therefore attract very close scrutiny and require very high standards of design.

FRED PILBROW KPF

This chapter describes the context, form and public realm considerations that inform the design of new tall buildings. Specifically, it:

↘ Discusses the relationship between the design of tall buildings and their context

↘ Considers the character of the built form and its impact at different distances

↘ Assesses what *quality* means in the conception and execution of tall buildings

↘ Evaluates how tall buildings can contribute to, or detract from, the public realm

↘ Describes how appropriately designed tall buildings can contribute to urban sustainability.

Available guidance

Local authorities in determining tall building proposals will generally seek the views of relevant consultees. CABE will review the quality of the architectural and urban design proposals and English Heritage will appraise their impact on heritage assets. These consultees' joint *Guidance on Tall Buildings* (2003) provides an overview of their criteria for assessing these proposals.

← Heron Tower, 110 Bishopsgate, designed by KPF, consented 2002: view from London Wall. The Heron Tower public inquiry provided the first opportunity to evaluate a tall building proposal against the joint criteria established by English Heritage and CABE, *Guidance of Tall Buildings*.
© Hayes Davidson/KPF

Context

'Context' embraces a building's physical setting and its social and economic environment. This section sets out pertinent considerations in appraising the impact of tall buildings on their context.

The urban realm

The skyline of British cities at the end of the nineteenth century was defined by buildings of civic or religious significance – by town halls, law courts and churches with their towers, domes and spires. A hundred years later, the visible pattern of cities is more complex. New buildings and infrastructure have recast the urban form and transformed the city skyline.

Recent tall building proposals represent the second or third generation of such buildings in British cities. The best of the earlier generations of these buildings provided quality pieces of architecture. Some of them are now protected by listing orders: Centrepoint – Grade II; BT Tower - Grade II; Trellick Tower – Grade II*.

However, these buildings' impact at street level and their relationships to the urban grain and city skyline were often less successful. Many tall buildings created space at their bases that was windswept and related poorly to surrounding patterns of activity. Tall buildings were often scattered across the city, rather than grouped so as to reinforce the city's visible structure and organisation.

The current policy framework for new tall building proposals and the proposals themselves draw on experience to avoid repeating such mistakes. The scope for tall buildings to make a positive contribution has been highlighted by CABE and others. This includes their potential to enhance a city by providing new points of orientation and focus, and to provide for an increase in urban density without sacrificing permeabilty of view and movement.

Tall building clusters

In the wider context of a city's skyline, there is now a broad consensus that tall buildings often look better in clusters. In this way they express the underlying

concentrations of activity and reinforce legibility in the urban realm.

The Royal Fine Art Commission, CABE's influential predecessor, shared this preference: 'a carefully arranged cluster of towers may be preferable to a number of isolated ones' (RFAC's 18th report, 1960–1962). The London Planning Advisory Committee's 1999 Guidance also emphasised the importance of reinforcing existing clusters of tall buildings. Recent proposals for tall

buildings have reinforced existing clusters whilst acknowledging the role that individual buildings play in the form of the cluster overall.

In London, such clusters now exist to the north east of the City of London, at Canary Wharf, Victoria, Paddington and London Bridge. The Mayor's London Plan also seeks to establish new tall building clusters to the east of the capital.

↖ View from Parliament Hill in 1999, showing Canary Wharf (to image left), the north eastern City cluster and the London Bridge cluster.
© KPF

← Policy guidance reinforces clusters as the preferred location for new tall buildings, shown in proposals for the enlarged north eastern City and London Bridge clusters.
© Eamonn O'Mahony

↓ The London Bridge Tower, designed by Renzo Piano Building Workshop, and consented in 2003, will form the nucleus of the London Bridge cluster.
© Hays Davidson & John Mclean

Siting tall buildings

Tall buildings are a significant presence in both their local environment and the city skyline. Their impact is therefore experienced over a wide area.

A site's relationship to heritage assets, open spaces and important views may preclude the acceptance of a tall building, because its scale would dominate or compromise the setting. The policy framework that has been developed for cities such as London provides guidance for considering these issues. The protection of important buildings and their settings has led to the establishment of controlled development planes such as the St Paul's Heights and the Strategic Views to St Paul's and the Palace of Westminster. A tall building proposed for London will be evaluated with respect to its impact on listed buildings, conservation areas, World Heritage Sites, the Royal Parks and other important open spaces and prospects, as well as the panoramas from the Thames' bridges and embankments.

The appropriateness or otherwise of a proposal for a tall building will inevitably be the subject of debate. The location of most urban sites is likely to imply some impact on heritage assets. In coming to a balanced appraisal, full and verifiably accurate information on which to make a decision is required.

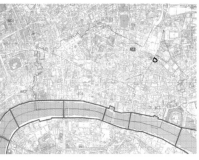

A tall building proposal in London would be assessed against its relationship to key urban conditions:

↑   River prospects and panoramas.
      © KPF

↑↑   Strategic Views and St Paul's Heights.
      © KPF

↘ In coming to a balanced appraisal, full and verifiably accurate information on which to make a decision is required.

↑   Listed buildings.
    © KPF

↑↑ Protected views to the Monument.
    © KPF

↑   World Heritage Sites.
    © KPF

↑↑ Conservation Areas.
    © KPF

↑   Scheduled Ancient Monuments.
    © KPF

↑↑ The Thames Policy Area.
    © KPF

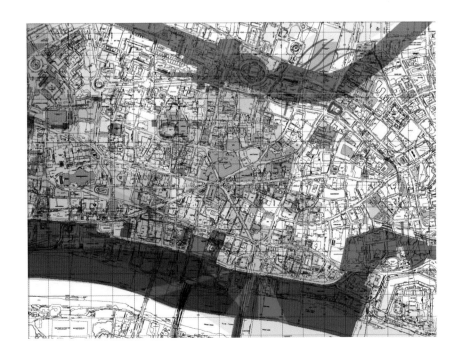

→   This overlay of constraints illustrates that the
    majority of sites in the City of London are
    constrained by one or more planning factors.
    © KPF

Evaluation tools

There is now a measure of consensus about how proposals for tall buildings should be technically evaluated. The planning process will require tall building applications to be accompanied by an Environmental Impact Assessment (EIA). This report will analyse the effects of the proposal on the environment. An assessment of potential townscape impacts undertaken as part of the EIA will require an applicant to identify the critical views impacted by the proposal. Applicants will then prepare these as verified photomontages. Particularly sensitive views may be rendered for different times of day and different seasons. These critical views need to be established early in the design process to assist the design team in determining the appropriate form and scale of their proposal.

Montages of the final proposal will allow an expert townscape consultant to appraise the impact of the proposal in the view. Such appraisals will be based on an assessment of the setting's qualities, the conservation area's character, or the listed building under consideration.

For the Heron Tower public inquiry, an independently verified computer model of the City of London was used by the architect as an essential tool to understand and appraise the impact of the new proposal on the existing environment and to analyse its impact in near and distant views. The model enabled accurate overlays to be made onto surveyed photographic backgrounds. Dialogue with the City of London Corporation and with statutory consultees established the critical townscape views to be assessed. These reflected the site's relationship to heritage assets, their settings and important views, prospects and panoramas. Over 130 verified views were prepared. Line views were supplemented by rendered montages that described the materials and coloration of the proposed building. Images were prepared for the most critical views in varying weather conditions and at different times of day. Models and mock-ups supplemented the view studies. This evidence demonstrated that the proposals conserved or enhanced the important heritage assets.

More technical detail of the process of townscape analysis can be found in the BCO publication, *Tall Buildings in London: Guidance on Planning* (2002).

← A selection of views prepared for the Heron Tower planning application by KPF, illustrating the building's relationship to St Paul's Cathedral.
© Hayes Davidson/KPF

↓ This verified computer model of the City of London provides a useful tool to appraise the potential townscape impacts of a tall building proposal. The model can establish where tall buildings would be visible at street level. The example shows, in red, where the lantern of St Paul's is visible from the surrounding streets.
© KPF

Regeneration

Context is economic as well as physical. Well designed and well sited tall buildings can promote urban prosperity.

Tall buildings have special potential to establish a new urban focus or enhance an existing building cluster. They can assist urban quarters in meeting the requirements of modern commerce, and help to define and strengthen urban

localities that are centered on particular activities.

Physically, tall buildings can act as beacons and vehicles for economic success. They signify prosperity and expand the supply of office space where there is occupier demand but scarcity of land or insufficient space suited to contemporary requirements and expectations. Visually, they have the potential to improve the appearance of city centres.

Social context

Context is also social, encompassing movement and activity. A good tall building will engage with the pattern of urban life.

Tall buildings offer the potential to create new public space at their base. Whether internal or external, this space should engage with its context, responding to established patterns of

The proposed London Bridge Tower, designed by Renzo Piano Building Workshop.

↓   Seen from Borough Market
     © Hayes Davidson & John Mclean

↘   Building section
     © Renzo Piano Building Workshop

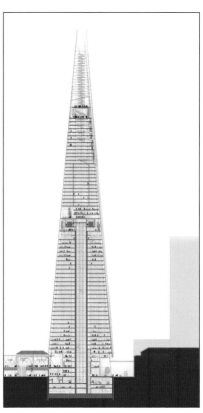

permeability, enclosure and movement.

Locating tall buildings at transport nodes provides for a critical mass of use and the economic potential associated with scale. This offers particular scope to invest in infrastructure, to create new public space and to enhance operations and urban amenities.

Where tall buildings provide for a mix of uses involving work, leisure, retail and/or residential functions, they can facilitate a reduction in urban travel. A mix of uses across clusters of tall buildings in close proximity to one another (with or without buildings of conventional height in the vicinity) also supports urban sustainability.

↓   Tall building proposals seen behind the Greater London Assembly building by Foster and Partners (to the foreground left) at London Bridge: London Bridge Tower, Renzo Piano Building Workshop (to the centre left) and New London Bridge House, KPF (to the centre right). Both proposals seek to address long-standing public realm shortcomings at London Bridge and to stimulate local regeneration. © GMJ

Built form
Constituents of form

The form of a tall building derives from its height, proportion and detailing. These work in combination to affect the building's impact. A tall building, rising above its surroundings, is perceived in the round. Its proportion – a function of both height and plan area – affects its impact on the townscape. For example, a building as high as Canary Wharf Tower may be acceptable in the context of the City of London, but one with an equivalent plan size and form in this area would almost certainly be contentious.

Form and distance

As tall buildings are seen in distant, middle and local views, their impact at these respective distances must be considered in the design development.

⬂ In distant views, the overall massing and proportion is most important. The relationship between the building's silhouette and the skyline should inform its design.

⬂ In mid-distance views, the building's overall composition and detail are perceived in balance. Here, the hierarchy and articulation of the elevations are particularly important.

⬂ The local views show the interrelationship between the building's base and its immediate setting. At this scale, the quality of materials and its detail is particularly critical.

↓ Heron Tower, 110 Bishopsgate. The articulation of the building façades, which reflect the variety of internal spaces, creates interest in mid-distance views. © KPF

↙ The design of tall buildings must respond to the varied scales at which they will be appreciated. The form of the Heron Tower, derived from its offset core, contributes to the overall form of the cluster in long views. © Hayes Davidson/KPF

↙↙ Local views will focus attention on the base of the building. A three-storey arcade on Bishopsgate responds to the scale of St Botolph's church opposite. © GMJ

↘ The form of a tall building derives from its height, bulk and detailing. A tall building, rising above its surroundings, is perceived in the round.

Form and orientation

The built form is also influenced by the building's orientation. The aspect, exposure to solar gain and prevailing wind patterns around the building should all influence its design. These functional considerations will influence the building's visual impact.

Form and the urban grain

A tall building's relationship to its urban context should influence its form. The building's massing may respond positively to its position in significant respects. For example, the Heron Tower's core position closes the vista along London Wall. The massing can also be tailored to keep the building from appearing in sensitive views. For example, the tapered form of 122 Leadenhall Street responds to views towards St Paul's along Fleet Street.

← Like a sculpture, tall buildings are seen in the round. Their form can respond to urban context, orientation and wind, minimising energy use and air turbulence.
© The Bridgeman Art Library/Getty Images

↓ The form of the Heron Tower responds to orientation and context. The building's appearance changes from different viewpoints around the city. The core, set to the south of the office floor plate, protects the accommodation from solar gain.
© Eamonn O'Mahony

Architectural quality

Recent decisions of public inquiries on tall buildings have emphasised the importance of architectural quality. The standards demanded of tall buildings generally are higher than those of low rise buildings, reflecting the relative visual prominence of tall structures.

Inadequate quality is a recognised failing of some early tall buildings in London which reflect weak standards of design, detailing and construction. Such failings are particularly significant because tall buildings often have a longer lifespan than their low rise equivalents. Both the initial level of investment in constructing a tall building, and the time and cost of demolition, tend to favour their retention. It is therefore prudent to plan tall buildings for a longer lifespan than a typical low rise building and to make a commensurate investment in their design and capital cost, to generate benefits of quality over the building's life.

Defining 'quality'

A high quality building is underpinned by the quality of both its conception and execution. Conceptual quality derives from a holistic design approach that encompasses context, technical integration and appropriate building form. Quality of execution – the building materials, workmanship and detail – helps in realising an effective conceptual strategy to produce a building whose performance and appearance will endure.

↑　30 St Mary Axe, designed by Foster and Partners

The design of the Swiss Re headquarters at 30 St Mary Axe creates a spiralling series of sky gardens within a smoothly profiled exterior. These apparently simple design elements, which are instantly recognisable in the finished building, address a number of separate issues. Externally, the circular form reduces the visual bulk of the building and its tapering base increases the public realm at ground level. The building's profile also reduces downdrafts.

Internally the sky gardens allow for regular 16.5m floor depths to be created within the changing building profile. The spiral offset of the sky gardens creates pressure differentials up the height of each of the sky gardens, allowing the offices to be naturally ventilated at certain times of year.

The detailing of the façade and its integration with the structure and services support the clarity of the building's concept.
© Nigel Young/Foster and Partners

↑　Heron Tower, 110 Bishopsgate, designed by KPF

London's first tall building designed for multi-tenancy challenges the orthodoxies of the central core and the separation of individual floors.

The core is located to the south of a floor plate that is arranged in three-storey 'villages' around a series of north-lit atria. Externally the building is articulated as 'served' and 'servant' spaces. The elevations relate to their respective contexts. The slender core terminates views along London Wall and Bishopsgate.

Internally, the building organisation supports its environmental performance. The core shields the floor plate from solar gain and the atria provide even daylight to the offices.
© Hayes Davidson/KPF

↑ Minerva Tower, Aldgate, designed by Grimshaw and Partners

The design concept for this 217m high, 43 storey building can be understood using the metaphor of four books facing one another with their covers open. Eight sheer façade planes, 1350 millimetre deep, form the 'covers'. No two covers ever meet, nor are they parallel. The ends reveal the individual sharpness and slenderness of each plane. Technically, each 1350 millimetre deep zone accommodates the primary structural stability frame and a naturally ventilated glass façade.

Four façade planes divide the site diagonally, creating a linear space that is broadest at its centre and narrower at its two ends. This serves as an entrance hall below and atrium above.

The building is asymmetric in section as well as in plan. Consequently no two elevations are the same and different aspects are revealed from different points of the compass.
© Smoothe Ltd.

↑ 122 Leadenhall Street, designed by Richard Rogers Partnership

The 47 storey, 220m high building clearly articulates the office accommodation, set into a tapering volume to the south and a slender service core to the north. The design provides for a high level of energy efficiency, flexible, efficient floor plates which maximise aspect and panoramic views. The megaframe concept provides a scaling device for the façade and a highly efficient structural solution. The building form preserves views of St Paul's Cathedral along Fleet Street and creates a dramatic silhouette on the skyline.

The design generates a large south-facing volume at ground level, with a raked ceiling profile. This large space captures and extends the existing public plaza, offering retail and café/restaurant facilities.
© Richard Rogers Partnership/CityScape

Conceptual quality

The four examples shown here demonstrate that there are many different valid conceptual approaches to the design of tall buildings.

Each of the buildings illustrated here adopts a strategy that provides a conceptual framework for design decisions. This framework informs the organisation, external expression, integration of structure, envelope and services, and the character of spaces within the building.

Quality of execution

The quality of a tall building's conception must be matched by the quality of its execution. The visual prominence of tall buildings calls for them to continue to look good over time. This requires care in design, specification and workmanship and a long design life for components.

Case study: Parkhaven, Rotterdam
The design of Parkhaven Tower in Rotterdam, Europe's tallest mixed-use building, was informed by the highly efficient Dutch construction industry.

↘ Design

The scale of the tower allowed every element to be custom-designed to optimise construction and performance.

↘ Specification

Parkhaven's cladding design specifically had to accommodate high wind loads, building movement and the building's complex geometry.

↘ Workmanship

Challenging conditions favour prefabrication. The site for a tall building is a very challenging environment in which to deliver quality. It is subject to frequent high wind speeds, delivery of materials is restricted, and time and space are at a premium. This highlights the relevance of pre-fabricated components. In Parkhaven, a number of strategies were devised to address these problems. Crane usage was minimised, with the future lift cores exploited for the vertical delivery of materials. As the site is on the River Maas, material could be brought directly by barge. Prefabrication of cladding, service risers and toilet pods provided maximum quality in minimum time.

↘ Design life – maintenance strategy

The building design must facilitate the maintenance and replacement of its components. However, because access in tall buildings will always be challenging, such components must have a long life. For the Parkhaven project, automated robots to clean the façade were engineered, based on a pioneering innovation for tall buildings in Japan. This facilitates more frequent cleaning of the façade and thereby extends its design life.

Innovation

Tall buildings have traditionally been a test-bed for innovations in the building industry. Innovations of this nature often percolate down the wider building industry, with tall buildings prompting solutions to established problems that also encompass other building types. Unitised cladding – where the glazing and its frame are delivered to the construction site as a prefabricated

panel – was first used on tall buildings in the United States to provide rapid enclosure to the building's interior, and to control building quality in the demanding environment of a tall building construction site.

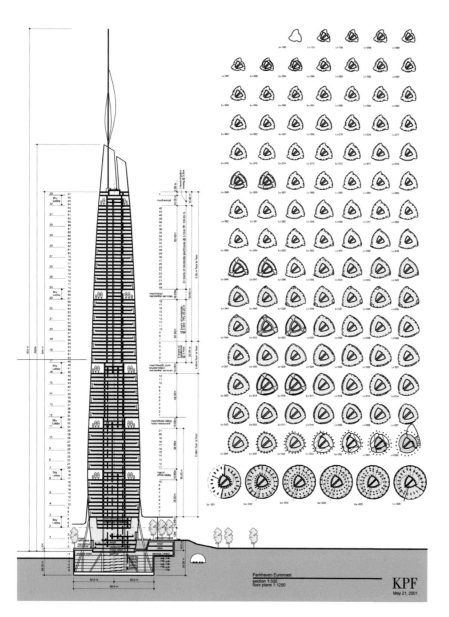

Proposals for Parkhaven, Rotterdam, designed by KPF 2003

←← Model demonstrating the interface between the building's structural form and cladding requirements.
© KPF

← Section and floorplans showing the design's exploitation of floor plate variation and the vertical distribution of different uses to optimise energy usage.
© KPF

Tall buildings can impact negatively on the
surrounding public realm, as evidenced in these
older examples.

    Centrepoint, Tottenham Court Road, London.
↑ © Justin Piperger

    New London Bridge House, London Bridge.
↗ © KPF

Tall buildings also have special potential to
contribute positively to the public realm at their
base, creating well designed amenity spaces for
enjoyable and comfortable public use.

→ Urban square at the base of HSBC, Hong Kong.
    © Ziona Strelitz

↘ The Rockefeller Centre, New York.
    © KPF

Public realm

How buildings meet the ground makes a significant impact on the public realm. The quality of the public realm in and around tall buildings encompasses the character of the spaces themselves and the activities they support. The engagement between these spaces and the surrounding city must be carefully judged in terms of their scale, character and permeability.

Earlier tall buildings, often conceived as hermetic and with minimal connection to the surrounding city, are now recognised to have been weak in engagement with their immediate context. Many tall buildings of this period were accessed by elevated pedestrian walkways. Centrepoint at the end of London's Tottenham Court Road is an example. The building is approached by an entrance stair that is set over water at the centre of a busy traffic gyratory. The result is a windy and hostile streetscape.

In contrast, recent proposals for tall buildings reflect careful social and environmental analysis, including analysis of movement patterns, the use of wind tunnel testing and computer simulations of overshadowing. This supports building engagement with the local context on more sociable terms.

Permeability

Good urban design offers a range of appropriately scaled public routes and spaces. The pressure to provide large floor plates through site amalgamation has closed some city routes, coarsening the urban grain. Tall buildings with smaller footprints offer the potential to create new routes through and around them. Visual connections can also be established through tall buildings. The predominant use of glass at lower levels opens up new vistas and affords visual links between the surrounding spaces. Examples include the proposed public concourses at the bases of 122 Leadenhall Street and the Heron Tower.

↘How buildings meet the ground makes a significant impact on the public realm. Recent proposals for tall buildings reflect careful environmental analysis, including the use of wind tunnel testing and computer simulations of overshadowing.

External public space

Tall buildings may offer opportunities to provide new public spaces. In contrast to low buildings with large floor plates, tall buildings can facilitate the reinstatement of the historic urban grain. Tall building footprints can be reduced because the area that is lost at ground level is balanced by new floor space at a greater number of upper levels. At 30 St Mary Axe, the building tapers in towards its base, enlarging the open area around it.

The scale of economic investment represented by a major tall building proposal may enable far-reaching reassessments of inherited traffic arrangements where public space has been dominated by vehicular traffic. The Heron Tower is set back from its site boundary to ease traffic constriction on Camomile Street, allowing for the pedestrianisation of Houndsditch.

The creation of new public space at major transport interchanges is both opportune and beneficial. For example, the New London Bridge House proposals bring forward a new bus station and public square at the entrance to London Bridge Station.

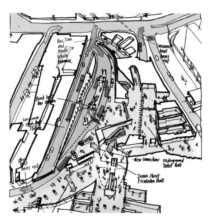

← ← Existing approach to the station, dominated by bus stands.
© KPF

← The new bus station relocated beneath the station concourse.
© KPF

↙ The creation of a new urban plaza in front of London Bridge Station.
© Frederic Terreaux

→ The proposals for the London Bridge Tower by Renzo Piano Building Workshop, consented in 2003, involve a finely detailed wind canopy that also serves to upgrade the entrances to London Bridge Station.
© GMJ

↘ Recent tall building proposals focus on the benefits of mixing building uses.

Internal public space

Traditionally, tall buildings in the UK were dedicated to a single use that limited the potential for public access. Recent tall building proposals focus on the benefits of mixing building uses.

The proposed London Bridge Tower extends public access up to viewing galleries at the top of the building. The proposals for 122 Leadenhall Street extend the activities of the street into the base of the building through a seven-storey high public foyer.

Public amenities

These can be used by the building's own occupants and enrich the range of facilities available to the wider community.

← The proposals for 122 Leadenhall Street, London, by Richard Rogers Partnership, consented in 2004, provide for permeability through the building base via a multi-level public winter garden that extends the existing external public plaza into the building.
© Richard Rogers Partnership/CityScape

↓ The proposals for the Heron Tower, 110 Bishospgate, London, by KPF provide for permeability at a high level inside the building, via a two-level public restaurant and bar on the top floors where the space will command 360 degree panoramic views over the city.
© GMJ

Microclimate

Tall buildings affect the microclimate of their surroundings. Appropriate measures must be taken during the design to ensure that these impacts are not harmful. Designers can refine their proposals with the aid of physical modelling such as wind tunnel tests and computer simulations.

Wind effects

Windiness at ground level relates to basic building mass and its relationship to surrounding buildings. Tall buildings can significantly change the wind environment in the surrounding streets. This can affect air quality in terms of dispersion of emissions from buildings or vehicles. Tolerance to wind relates to the activities undertaken in the setting. Acceptable conditions for a pedestrian street are not necessarily appropriate to café life. Excessive infiltration to the building through doors or other openings must also be avoided.

→   Proposals for Parkhaven, Rotterdam, KPF 2003, showing the building form designed to minimise surrounding turbulence.
© KPF

↓   Wind effects of tall buildings which impact on the external setting can be accurately prediced by wind tunnel tests, shown here for the Heron Tower, at RWDI, Toronto.
© Arup

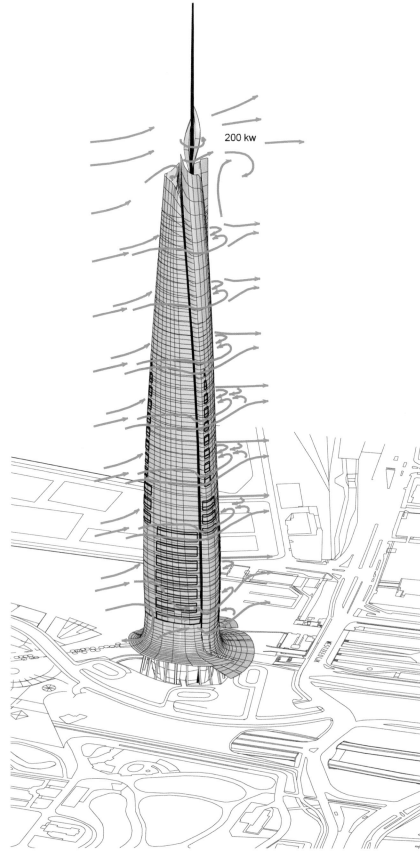

200 kw

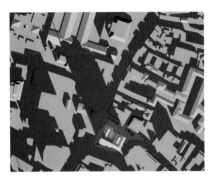

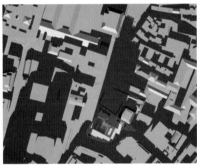

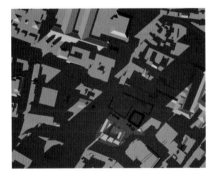

↖   Shadow study, Heron Tower.
      © KPF

Sunlight, daylight and shadowing
Tall buildings inevitably create a degree of overshadowing. Evaluating this impact involves a number of considerations.

As part of a planning application, the timing and duration of any overshadowing will be considered in relation to established patterns of use. A tall building that overshadows a public space early in the morning when the space is not intensively used is more acceptable than one that overshadows it at lunchtime. Residential amenity will also be a consideration, with any reduction in levels of sunlight and daylight needing to conform to established Building Research Establishment guidelines.

Established rights of light will also inform the design, with well developed civil law rights protecting the interests of owners and occupiers. Unacceptable impacts may result in redress by the courts, with an injunction to stop the works.

Reflected solar glare and night time light pollution are further considerations. Sunlight, daylight and overshadowing effects in relation to tall buildings are discussed in greater depth in the BCO publication *Tall Buildings in London: Guidance on Planning* (2002).

↘ Designers can refine their proposals with the aid of physical modelling such as wind tunnel tests and computer simulations.

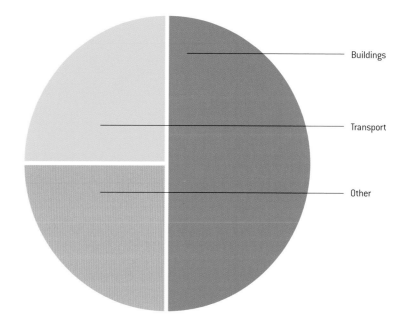

Buildings

Transport

Other

→   The comparative output of CO_2 emissions
    by buildings, transport and other uses.
    Given that buildings are responsible for
    almost 50% of CO_2 emissions in the UK
    (Department of Environment, Food and
    Rural Affairs), and that transport
    contributes a further 25% of annual
    emissions, reducing these emissions by
    appropriately sited and well designed tall
    buildings is important.
    © KPF

Energy

Although aspects of tall building operation are inherently energy intensive, tall building proposals are required to meet ambitious, newly intensified sustainability targets. As buildings account for almost 50% of carbon dioxide emissions in the UK (Department for Environment, Food and Rural Affairs), the scope for building design and operations to reduce this is vital.

Traditionally, the energy costs associated with vertical transportation systems, the requirements to distribute building services, and the high wall-to-floor ratios of tall buildings all mitigated against low energy usage in these structures. Recent proposals have demonstrated that with integrated design and use of the modelling tools now available, the energy usage of tall buildings can be reduced, without compromising occupant comfort.

Controlling light and air

Tall buildings have the potential for excellent daylighting characteristics, particularly, in small floor plate buildings where the whole floor can be within 9–12m of the façade. As well as providing better environmental quality for people in the building, generous daylight provision reduces dependence on artificial lighting with its attendant energy costs. Designers must consider the floor to ceiling height in respect of type, position and proportion of glazing relative to the floor plan, especially in larger floor plate buildings where the clear height from floor to ceiling, and the edge treatment on the perimeter of the floor, affect the environmental experience of people on the deeper parts of the floor.

As all individuals do not want the same internal conditions, a degree of individual control is appropriate. Recent developments in façade design facilitate

natural ventilation in tall buildings. Active multi-layered façades allow air to be drawn in from the exterior in a controlled manner, allowing parts of the building to function without air-conditioning at appropriate times of year, and affording a degree of individual control.

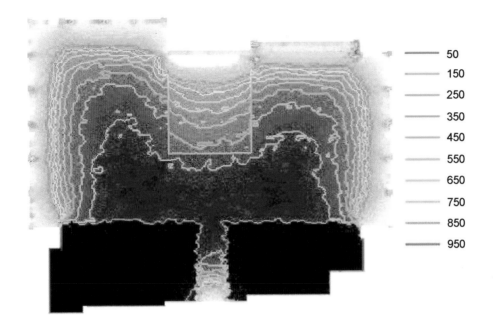

─────	50
─────	150
─────	250
─────	350
─────	450
─────	550
─────	650
─────	750
─────	850
─────	950

← The proposals for the Heron Tower, 110 Bishopsgate, involve north facing atria that provide excellent natural daylight to the office workspace inside the building, thereby minimising the energy required for artificial lighting.
© KPF

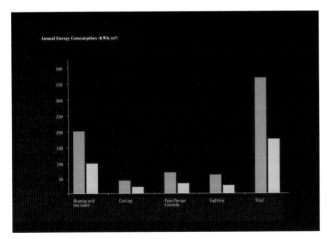

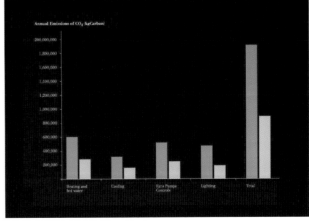

↑ The proposals for the Heron Tower, 110 Bishopsgate, enable the building's planning, façade and services design to deliver excellent environmental performance, utilising less than half the energy requirements of a standard air-conditioned building, with annual CO_2 emissions less than half those of a comparable sized air-conditioned building.
© KPF

Outwich Street   Bishopsgate

building performance:
design development

↘**Integrated design:** The chapter outlines the key technical parameters of tall buildings. The systems for tall buildings are different in their scale, order and interrelationships from those for buildings of conventional height. Successful design is based on appropriate development of the component systems. This is achieved by the range of specialist consultants shaping their respective proposals and the overall synthesis of elements, collaboratively, through iterative design. The final proposal should integrate the individual components in an optimal solution to meet the objectives for the building.

ZIONA STRELITZ ZZA

The overriding aim is provision of an efficient floor plate and an effective internal environment. The critical parameters for efficient design are storey height and size of both the floor plate and core. The vertical transportation design is a critical driver, with implications for the structure, design and positioning of the core and the distribution of the building's mechanical systems. Lift design is a major determinant of the core size, the net to gross floor area ratio, the potential for space planning and the future adaptability of the accommodation.

Each of the building's systems impinge on the totality. With increasing height, the choice of component systems for structure, mechanical, cladding and life safety systems increases, as does the range of potential design solutions. For example, the designers of a building of 15 storeys would probably serve the building by a single group of conventional lifts, whereas at 60 storeys, zoned banks, with single- or double-deck cars, transfer floors and sky lobbies, and combinations of high speed shuttles and local lift groups become relevant, and permutations of these alternatives requiring evaluation.

← Heron Tower, 110 Bishopsgate, designed by KPF, consented 2002
East-west section, illustrating integrated provision for internal space, lifts, structure, services, envelope and life safety.
© KPF

Fred Pilbrow
KPF

Arranging the building
Interior space

The interior of a tall building will reflect the anticipated demands of its future occupants. The configuration of the desired floor plate may need to be reconciled with the constraints of the site. If deep plan space is sought on a constricted site, the cores may be set to the edge of the floor plate. Conversely, if shallower depth perimeter space is required, the core may be set at the centre of the floor plate.

Size of floor plate

The size of available sites and the planning constraints on low bulky buildings limit the potential for very large floor plates in traditional city centres. Tall buildings therefore offer organisations scope to consolidate in single buildings in traditional city centres. Other occupiers are attracted to larger floor plates which are feasible at peripheral sites like Canary Wharf. These have proved attractive to large occupiers such as financial institutions.

Sub-tenancy

Tall buildings should be designed to facilitate sub-tenancies on all but the smallest floor plates (i.e. those less than 600m²). Ideally the floor plate should allow flexibility for future leasing arrangements without prescribing the exact size of a potential sub-tenancy. It should offer occupants leasing an entire floor a regular continuous working space.

Comparison of floor plates and core configurations in a selection of tall buildings in London, presented at similar scale and north orientation.

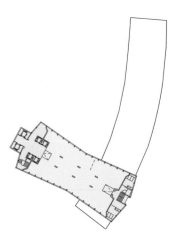

→   New London Bridge House, London Bridge 1967, Richard Seifert and Partners.
© Richard Seifert and Partners (redrawn by KPF)

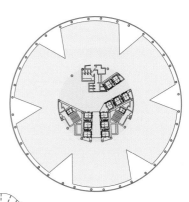

→   30 St Mary Axe, Swiss Re, completed 2004, Foster and Partners.
© Foster and Partners (redrawn by KPF)

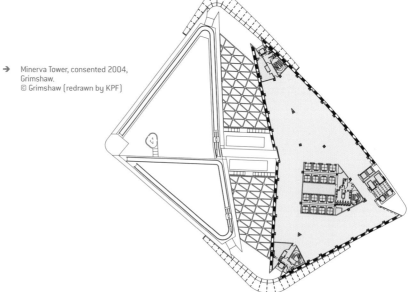

→   Minerva Tower, consented 2004, Grimshaw.
© Grimshaw (redrawn by KPF)

The building illustrated vary in size, depth and shape, as well as in their sectional arrangements. This diversity reflects these designs' response to their contexts and the varied requirements of occupier organisations.

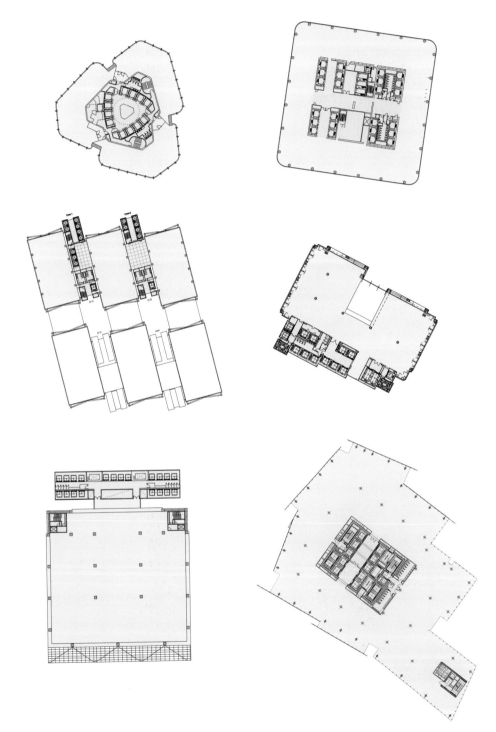

← HSBC Canary Wharf, completed 2002, Foster and Partners.
© Foster and Partners (redrawn by KPF)

←← Tower 42, 1980, Richard Seifert and Partners.
© Richard Seifert and Partners (redrawn by KPF)

← Heron Tower, 110 Bishopsgate, consented 2002, KPF.
© KPF

←← Grand Union Building, Paddington, consented 2004, Richard Rogers Partnership.
© Richard Rogers Partnership (redrawn by KPF)

← London Bridge Tower, consented 2003, Renzo Piano Building Workshop.
© Renzo Piano Building Workshop (redrawn by KPF)

←← 122 Leadenhall Street, consented 2004, Richard Rogers Partnership.
© Richard Rogers Partnership (redrawn by KPF)

In their different ways, the designs address contemporary design objectives for good tall buildings: maximising landlord efficiency, maximising external aspect, providing flexibility for occupiers' internal space planning, providing good spatial quality, and minimising energy usage whilst contributing to environmental quality in the workspace.

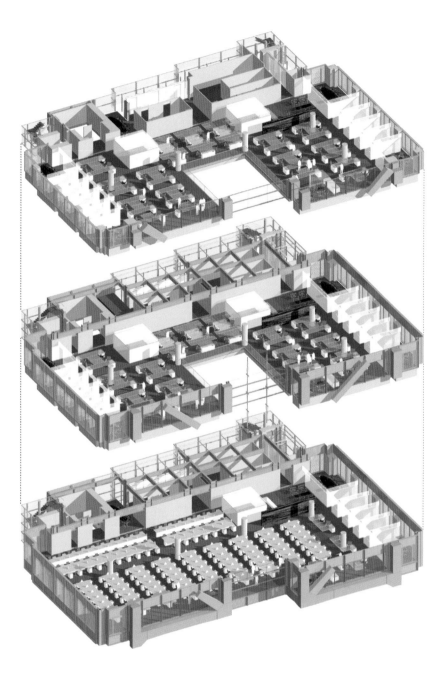

Depth of floor plate

Occupier requirements for floor depths vary greatly. Smaller, shallow floor plates provided in refurbished, first generation tall buildings have attracted smaller tenants and tenants seeking a high percentage of cellularisation. However, large tenants seek the flexibility associated with deeper floors which allow for varied and adaptable working modes. Recent tall building proposals in London have provided different floor plate configurations – sometimes in a single building, to cater for occupiers' varied needs.

↑ Heron Tower, 110 Bishopsgate: axonometric of office 'village'. Deep plan floors are interspersed with pairs of shallower gallery floors to form three-storey independent clusters up the building's height. The quality of workspace for the Heron Tower was a key driver in the design. Research into tenant experience of the space in existing tall buildings such as Tower 42 suggested a preference for an open and adaptable working environment. The offset core arrangement of the Heron Tower, allied to the 'village organisation' of the floor plates, offers such flexibility. The building is designed as a bespoke multi-let building, offering occupants a range of tenancy sizes, from half of a single floor to a 'village' of three levels, enabling tenants to interlink individual floors. The atrium at the heart of the cluster provides a social focus. Each cluster or 'village' offers a range of floor plate depths as well as the potential for inter-connection between floors within a tenant's demise.
© KPF

The section

The sectional height of a tall building will be determined by the spaces allocated to the occupied zone, the services and structure.

The sectional height of the occupied zone will be set by factors such as the floor plate depth, intended use, daylight penetration and arrangements for building servicing. Deeper floors need taller ceilings. Some activities, such as trading operations that benefit from a raked floor with clear sight lines, may require an increased floor-to-ceiling height.

An adequately sized services zone – typically below a raised floor and above a suspended ceiling – is important to accommodate power, data and environmental services. The size of the structural zone will be a function of the building's span. Commonly, structural and services zones are overlapped – with services penetrating the structural beams.

The section of a tall building does not have to be repetitive up the building's height. Recently designed tall buildings include larger volume atria that interconnect groups of floors. These taller spaces serve as buffer areas to allow for

natural ventilation, as well as creating spatial variety inside the building. A social benefit of such spaces is the scope they offer for interaction between people based on different floors above ground level.

A combination of express and local lifts offers additional opportunities to vary a building's sectional treatment. Sky lobbies – where local and express lifts connect – can be defined as public or semi-public spaces, beyond which access can be restricted. For example, an occupier above a sky lobby can locate the organisation's reception area at this elevated level.

Commerzbank, Frankfurt, completed 1997, Foster and Partners. Offices are arranged around a spiral of wintergardens. These landscaped areas are interconnected up the height of the building to facilitate its mixed-mode environmental strategy. The base of the wintergardens provides breakout spaces for the adjacent offices.
← © Nigel Young/Foster and Partners
↓ © Foster and Partners

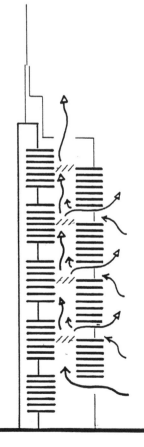

Core distribution

Cores in tall buildings are more complex than in buildings of conventional height and their design is fundamental both to space efficiency and the building's operational effectiveness. Vertical circulation, services distribution and support functions for the floor plate (bathrooms, cleaners' cupboards and, in some cases, on-floor plant) are typically grouped in cores. The functions may be gathered into a single core or distributed to a number of smaller cores. The cores may be sited at the building's centre or its perimeter.

The core and the floor plate

Concentrating support functions in the core frees up the remaining accommodation allowing the space to be replanned more easily in the event of changing occupier needs. The position of the core shapes the usable space of the building. Its location should therefore reflect the nature of the space that is desired.

Centre core arrangements

Placing the core at the centre of the building will create a ribbon of usable space between the core and the building's perimeter. The relative sizes of the site and the core will determine the depth of this usable space. Tall buildings planned in the 1960s generally followed this arrangement, with shallow floor depths of 6-8m. These buildings' small floor plates reflected the constraints of the established urban grain, the difficulty of assembling larger plots, and the lack of pressure from occupier organisations for large floor plates to accommodate their operations. More recent buildings at Canary Wharf, which were not similarly constrained, have expanded core to wall depths to 13.5m.

Two recent tall building proposals combine a radial plan with a tapered section. Their respective internal spaces differ as a consequence of their contrasting core locations.

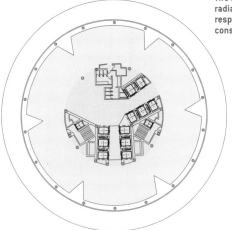

30 St Mary Axe, London, Foster and Partners.

↑   © Centralphotography.com

↖   The plan with its centre core provides
↙   even depth space throughout the floor
    plate.
    © Foster and Partners
    (redrawn by KPF)

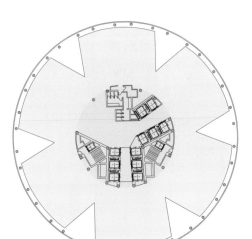

Torre Agbar, Barcelona, designed by Ateliers Jean Nouvel.

↗   The elevation of the curved form is
    enriched by the pattern of
    fenestration.
    © Ateliers Jean Nouvel

↘   The plan's offset core provides a range
    of floor plate sizes, space-planned
    here for a medium density use.
    © Ateliers Jean Nouvel

↘↘ The external reference points show the
    sense of connection from the building
    interior to the fabric of the city.
    © Ateliers Jean Nouvel

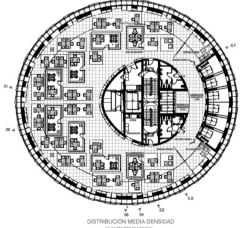

DISTRIBUCIÓN MEDIA DENSIDAD
ocupación total 47 personas

DISTRIBUCIONES PLANTA TIPO.
00   02   05   10

01. Parque Güell
02. Sagrada Família
03. Mar Mediterráneo
04. Parque de la Ciudadela
05. Barceloneta
06. Puerto Olímpico
07. Mediterráneo

The central core arrangement offers several advantages in a tall building:

- It maximises the usable space at the building's perimeter, allowing a greater proportion of the workspace to be naturally lit

- It places the core in a structurally efficient location where it can provide for the building's stability

- It allows for efficient sub-division of the floor plate to accommodate two or more sub-tenancies on a floor without sacrificing usable space.

Offset core arrangement

The centre core arrangement will not suit every occupier or every site. It breaks up the floor plate by blocking views and access across its centre. Central cores may be particularly inappropriate on small sites where the resulting depth of floor would be inflexibly small. Many potential sites do not offer outlook in all directions and cores may be planned adjacent to party walls where workspace would be compromised. The core's role in providing stability will only be effective for structures of medium height, beyond which structure in the building's perimeter zone becomes necessary.

Cores may be set at the edge of the floor plate – either in one location or distributed at a number of smaller satellites. This arrangement frees the usable accommodation from the obstructions of the fixed service risers. The resultant floor plate is deeper and allows views and access across its centre. Recent projects have exploited the offset core arrangement for environmental benefits. These include shading the usable accommodation with the core and allowing access to ventilation for on-floor plant.

Adrian Godwin
Lerch Bates & Associates

Vertical transportation
Design objectives

The design of the vertical transportation services for tall buildings is critical. Lifts for passengers and goods are the building's 'life blood'. Failure to make adequate provision would lead to difficulties in servicing the building, rendering it operationally deficient. However, over-provision results in excessive capital cost and the loss of lettable area forever, with the resultant impact on the building's capital value.

The design criteria for vertical transportation systems have not varied substantially in the last 50 years. The two fundamental criteria for lifts in office buildings are quality and quantity of service.

Target standards

The basic service requirements generally target an average interval of 30 seconds, and a 5-minute handling capacity for 12-15% of the building population in morning peak traffic up the building. This necessitates a realistic view of the projected population before a tall building's vertical circulation can be designed. It also requires consideration of local occupational densities, operational uses and building occupancy, with allowances for holidays, sickness and the projected pattern of arrivals and departures.

Guidelines provided in the BCO Specification apply to tall office buildings as well as to buildings of conventional height. However, consideration may need to be given to other factors in tall buildings, such as the potential for occupational density to diminish on floors higher up the building. The reduced density relates to the higher space being more prestigious, and therefore less densely occupied.

← The double-deck lifts for the proposed Heron Tower, designed by KPF, optimise transportation and floor plate efficiency. The glazed lifts positioned on the external elevation animate the public realm whilst providing views out for passengers.
© Hayes Davidson/KPF

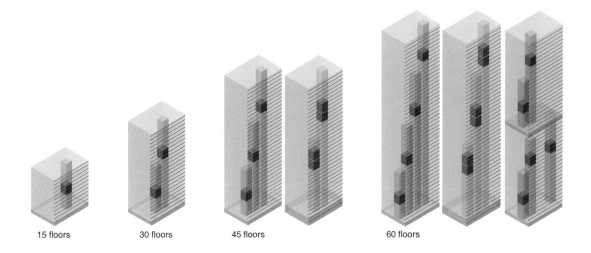

15 floors   30 floors   45 floors   60 floors

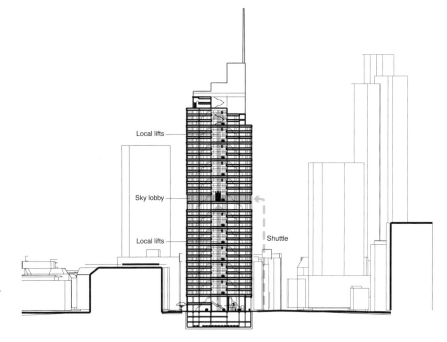

Local lifts

Sky lobby

Local lifts

Shuttle

↑   Possible lifting scenarios for buildings of 15, 30, 45
    and 60 storeys, reflecting the increased options for
    providing efficient lift service to taller buildings, via
    single-deck, double-deck or a sky lobby lift
    installation.
    © KPF

→   Heron Tower, 110 Bishopsgate, designed by KPF, for
    which various lifting permutations were tested
    during design development. The scheme shown
    above explores the creation of a sky lobby at the
    centre of the building, allowing the high rise and low
    rise lift shafts to be stacked. This was abandoned in
    favour of a double-deck lift proposal.
    © KPF

Lift strategy

In tall buildings, the main components of
the lift strategy are the number of lifts
per group, and the number of lift zones.
A typical strategy is to divide a building
into a number of zones, each served by
an appropriately sized group of lifts.
Specialist input is required to achieve
the right balance between number of
zones, size of groups, core size and lift
performance, in order to meet cost, area
and performance objectives.

Conventionally the maximum number of
lifts in a single group would be eight,
with each group normally serving up to
15-18 floors. Accordingly, a 45-storey
office building with a large floor plate will
typically require three groups of lifts,
serving low, mid and high rise zones, in
addition to goods and fire fighting lifts.

On buildings above 50-60 storeys, the
size of the lift core required to serve all
floors directly from the ground floor
becomes prohibitive. As an alternative,
sky lobbies served by express lifts can
be introduced, reducing the overall
number of lift shafts travelling through
the lower parts of the building. The space
taken up by lift cores can be reduced by

a further 30% through the adoption of
double-deck lifts, although these require
the introduction of carefully designed
two-level lift lobbies, both at ground and
sky lobby levels.

Predicting lift traffic

During the last twenty years, more
design tools have been available to
analyse and investigate the predicted
performance of vertical transportation
systems, including computer simulation
techniques. Traffic peaks for incoming,
inter-floor and outgoing traffic can now
be studied to see where unacceptably

degraded performance will be likely to occur first. If facilities such as restaurants are to be placed on a building's upper floors, the design should take account of this at an early stage. Such a significant facility will have a considerable impact on the lift traffic patterns, in contrast to the generic situation where, apart from general interfloor traffic, all traffic emanates to and from the main building lobby.

Destination hall call

The advent of 'destination hall call' control systems enables passengers to 'book' their destination floor electronically when they are in the lobby and before they enter a lift. This has the potential for more efficient lift systems. In certain circumstances, the number of lifts installed can be reduced compared to the traditional 'two button group collective control systems'.

An advantage of destination hall call control systems is the additional flexibility it gives to the layout and arrangement of groups of lifts:

- ↘ Use of more than eight lifts in one group if required
- ↘ Placing lifts in one group with their entrances in line
- ↘ Arranging lifts in the same group in two distinct lobbies
- ↘ Handling more than the typical 15-18 floors by one group of lifts.

Analysis for these types of control systems requires traffic simulation programs.

Mixed use design

For mixed use buildings, including hotel, apartment, public amenity and office uses, each component use must be analysed with the traffic design criteria that pertain to the types of traffic peak typically experienced in such facilities. Logical stacking usually places the least densely populated uses in the highest part of the building, e.g. apartments at the top, hotel in the middle, and offices at the building base. Having fewer people to transport to the higher levels of the building is advantageous as it generates less demanding requirements for the size of lift core.

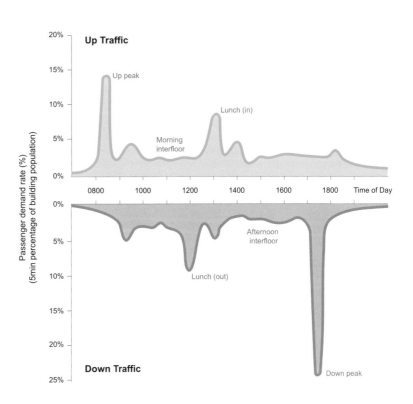

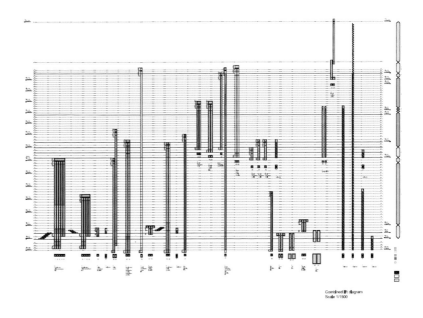

Combined lift diagram
Scale 1/1500

↑↑ Predicted lift traffic distribution over the course of a typical day.
© Lerch Bates Associates

↑ Lift schematic, London Bridge Tower, designed by Renzo Piano Building Workshop, reflecting the vertical transport strategy for passengers, freight and fire fighting in a mixed use building which typically provides separate lift services for each of the constituent parts.
© Lerch Bates Associates

Average journey time

In low rise office buildings of up to 16 floors or so, it is not unusual to find one group of lifts serving the entire building, with each lift in the group serving all the upper office floors. Once buildings exceed 16-18 floors – if overall population levels do not require this before – splitting the floors into two or more zones, or serving contiguous sets of floors by separate groups of lifts, will

be considered to meet the design criterion of 'average journey time'. Some lift solutions for a proposed building may meet the quoted requirement for quality and quantity of lift service, but involve an excessive average journey time. This would be caused by too much travel distance, combined with too many stops within the zone. An effective criterion for tall buildings is to limit average journey time to around 90 to 100 seconds. Double-deck lifts may

well be worth considering in tall buildings of 50 floors or more, although sometimes in buildings with fewer floors if over 100 people per floor are anticipated.

Single versus double-deck

In cities where land prices are very high and the typical footprint of buildings is relatively small, e.g. in Singapore, double-deck lifts are often used to save

core space (both the number and/or size of cores). Control systems for double-deck lift installations are becoming more sophisticated. 'Destination hall call' control systems may soon be applied to double-deck lifts, following their now successful use with single-deck lifts. Typically, the maximum zone size for double-deck lifts is around 24 floors, compared to 15 to 18 floors for single-deck. The reasons relate to average journey time. A rough rule of

thumb for the ratio of double- to single-deck lifts to service a given building is two-thirds. Whilst the capital cost of the double-deck lifts is higher than for single-deck lifts, the overall vertical transportation costs may be similar because fewer double-deck lifts are required. The major difference is that the double-deck solution enables valuable net lettable space to be recovered.

↘ In cities where land prices are very high and the typical footprint of buildings is relatively small, e.g. in Singapore, double-deck lifts are often used to save core space.

← Two banks of glazed panoramic double-decks serve the Heron Tower. Entry from the building lobby is at ground and first floor level, with separate access to lower ground. There is also separate lift access to the public facilities at the top of the building. Heron Tower, 110 Bishopsgate, designed by KPF, consented 2002.
© GMJ

Planning considerations

Height and complexity

As building height increases above about 50 floors, and single-deck lifts can potentially exceed four groups of eight lifts, the question arises of how best to serve additional floors. Continuing with conventional single-deck solutions reduces area on the lower floors by necessitating too many lift shafts.

The use of sky lobbies is an important device for tall and very tall buildings. They provide for a series of non-stop shuttle lifts to move substantial portions of the building population – typically those occupying the building's upper portion – directly to a sky lobby. From the sky lobby, the users transfer to 'local' lifts, either single or double-deck. These can service local zones above or below each sky lobby. This system saves space. As the express shuttle lifts are non-stop, they can move many people in express fashion from the main building lobby to an upper sky lobby. This is efficient, involving fewer lifts than a system which emanates from the main lobby to deliver people to their final destination floor.

The handling capacity of shuttle lifts can be increased by using double-deck and loading passengers from dual-stacked main floor lobbies. The use of 'through cars' with front and rear openings can also aid passenger throughput and handling capacity by allowing simultaneous boarding and alighting.

There are three notional varieties of sky lobby: 'conventional', 'top/down' and 'up/down' arrangements. The sky lobby type is designated by the way users transfer to the 'local' lifts, the direction of the local lift service and the local zone from the sky lobby. This can be 'up' from the sky lobby (conventional), 'down' from the sky lobby, or 'up and down' from the sky lobby, the latter involving at least two zones of local lifts.

Future trends

Getting more performance from fewer lifts is key to future lift technology. Future development of very tall buildings – 120 floors or more – will necessitate more efficient vertical transportation solutions than currently exist. This is likely to focus on running multiple shuttle cars in one lift shaft, given that use of a single lift car in one shaft to shuttle people to a sky lobby in a very tall building is inefficient. Such systems have already been designed on paper. Market demand for cost-effective solutions should create opportunities to design and test the first prototypes. The 'return on investment case' to implement such systems has already been made.

Recent events have led to greater consideration of safe, effective evacuation by lift. This is technically feasible. The necessary development for its adoption is in building management and occupant training, and adaptation of building codes and regulations.

→ Planning considerations: The mnemonic SPACE summarises the five most important factors in designing lift solutions for tall buildings.

↘ Getting more performance from fewer lifts is key to future lift technology.

Space

The most fundamental requirement is to minimise the floor space taken by vertical transportation. This will ensure that the maximum net lettable area results. However, the solution adopted must not compromise any of the other four factors.

Ease of use

In order for the solution to succeed for building users, a number of performance requirements must be met. This includes good signage, acceptable journey times, minimal walking distances, minimal transfers between shuttle and local lifts, logical arrangement of lobbies and simplicity of design.

Performance

The typical criteria for traffic performance, i.e. 5-minute group handling capacity and average interval as well as average journey time, need to be met.

Architectural fit

The arrangement of the cores and circulation spaces, and the balance between the design intent for the building and the lift solution, need to be maintained to support the building's architectural concept.

Capital cost

Consistent with meeting other design requirements, capital cost should be minimised, e.g. by not over-specifying requirements such as speed, and always designing for the minimum number of lift entrances per floor, using the smallest number of cars within a given group.

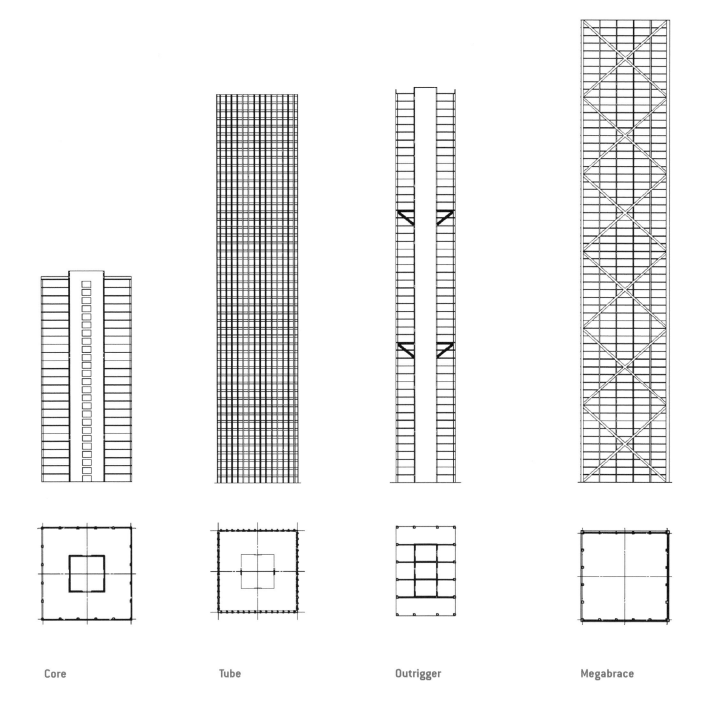

Core

Tube

Outrigger

Megabrace

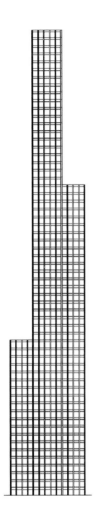

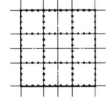

Bundled tube

← Alternative structural strategies to
provide tall building stability.
© Arup

Harry Bridges
Arup

Structural systems
Structural form

The structure is the building's 'skeleton' which is required to perform a variety of functions. It should provide effective floor plates, facilitate vertical circulation and mechanical and electrical distribution, and support the building's functions within an effective form. The structural form should contribute to the buildings character and identity, while being efficient, cost effective and 'construction friendly'.

An efficient generic theme for tall structures is to arrange for the structural form which provides sway resistance to support as high a proportion of the building mass as possible. This way, the same structural material performs in supporting vertical load and resisting lateral sway. The building mass is also mobilised to resist overturning.

The greater the building height, the wider the structural form needs to be to reach up to that height and perform well under lateral loads. These characteristics can be seen in the illustrative forms (left): the effective 'structural width' increases with height. The structure's location in the building changes to provide the greater width required.

At medium heights, the primary form can be a core around the lifts, stairs and risers. As height increases, this tends to be too narrow to provide effective sway resistance; the next logical location for the structural form is to explore the use of the building perimeter. There are many different approaches to this, illustrated in the diagrams to the left.

Good design takes advantage of historic experience, combined with innovative approaches and new ideas. Iterative steps can be taken in design, supported by parametric studies to substantiate new ideas. These steps derive the technical, functional and aesthetic aspects, to arrive at an assembly of preferred and reasoned choices for a building and its structural form.

The appropriate solution is devised in response to site conditions, design aims and project objectives. The following projects illustrate the range of structural strategies adopted in recent tall building projects.

↘ Good design takes advantage of historic experience, combined with innovative approaches and new ideas.

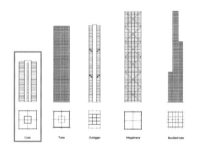

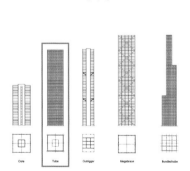

Centre core:

HSBC, Canary Wharf, London, designed by Foster and Partners; Structural Engineers, Arup.
→   Both © CentralPhotography.com

Tube:

Commerzbank HQ, Frankfurt, Germany, designed by Foster and Partners; Structural Engineers, Arup.
→   Both © Arup

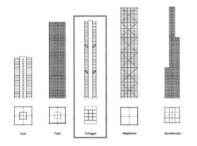

Outrigger:

International Financial Centre 2, Hong Kong,
designed by Cesar Pelli; Structural Engineers, Arup.
➜ Both © Arup

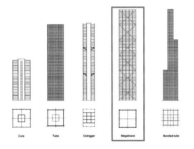

Megabrace:

Bank of China, Hong Kong, designed by IM Pei;
Structural Engineers, Leslie E. Robertson Associates.
➜ © Jeff Smith/Getty Images
➜➜ © Ziona Strelitz

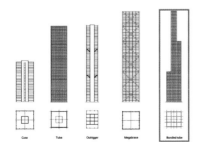

Bundled tube:

Sears Tower, Chicago, Skidmore, Owings & Merrill
LLP Architects and Structural Engineers.
➜ © Skidmore, Owings & Merrill LLP
➜➜ © Timothy Hursley

Stability assessment

The chosen structural form will be the subject of a strategic stability assessment, for both strength and stiffness, that may start with an overview and parametric studies, including modular subdivisions of a large form. A detailed 3-dimensional analytical model would be developed to optimise and substantiate the structural form and its material content for resistance to vertical loads and wind effects. Both the structure's static and dynamic characteristics will be substantiated.

For tall buildings a balance is sought between site constraints, building shape, space planning, aesthetics and structural form. The structure plays a critical part in this. To utilise the site effectively and provide an elegant form, the structure may be slender and hard working. This can lead to second order effects for the structure, such as sway P-d effects and oscillation under wind loads. These become more prominent with height, and need to be evaluated to achieve acceptable performances. Residential accommodation tends to need more stringent criteria against these effects than a busy office environment. This can be relevant in a building for mixed uses. The primary variable here is the structural form. Thereafter, such effects can be accommodated by sufficient material content to provide stiffness, or by adding deliberate damping into the building to mitigate lateral acceleration and the perception of this effect.

30 St Mary Axe, London

↗   Analytical 3D model of the tube structure, illustrating
     force and deflection with proposed building.
     © Arup

↓   © Nigel Young/Foster and Partners

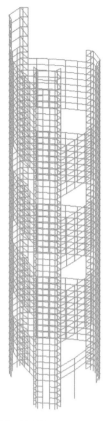

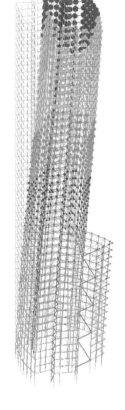

Commerzbank HQ, Frankfurt, Germany

Analytical structural model of the primary stability structure.

↗ © Arup

↓ © Ian Lambot

New London Bridge House, London Bridge

Analytical structural model of New London Bridge House showing buliding deflection.

↗ © Arup

↓ © GMJ

Structural materials

The choice of structural material goes hand in hand with the search for an effective structural form. In broad terms, steel is generally light and prefabricated, lending itself to speedy construction of tall structures while mitigating demands on foundations.

Trends in concrete involving high strengths, mechanised formwork, post-tensioning and prefabricated reinforcement cages provide effective structures. The material has inherent fire resistance and can provide soffits that can take finishes or partition heads directly. It is most effective in compression. However, concrete structures tend to be heavier and slower to construct.

Effective structural forms harness the strengths of material characteristics. There are examples of good choices which are all steel or all concrete. An increasing trend is to use the best of both, in a 'composite material' approach to the structure. Skills and economics vary geographically, and familiarity with, and testing in, the local construction environment are crucial steps in selecting optimal materials.

Structural materials used in tall buildings construction:

Steel:

Century Tower Tokyo, Japan, Foster and Partners, completed 1991. The structural form and material produce a light and ductile structural frame, to resist potential seismic activity.

↑   © Ian Lambot

↗   © Arup

Concrete:

Adia, Abu Dhabi, KPF 2005. Concrete was selected for the structural frame of Adia in response to the availability of local skills and comparative economic cost.

↖↑ © KPF both images

Steel and concrete:

Commerzbank, Frankfurt, Germany, Foster and Partners, completed 1997. Steel is good at tension and at producing long frames. Concrete is good in compression. Commerzbank contains the best of steel and high grade concrete.

←← © Arup both images

Floor systems

Floor systems tend to make up most of a building's weight. They can pose quite varied and different characteristics and are key to providing effective floor plates. Choices are influenced by floor spans, co-ordination of services and structural zones, and environmentally sustainable criteria such as provision of thermal mass and reduction of embodied energy. The following is a range of options:

Steel/metal deck and composite concrete topping

- ↘ Rolled sections
  Involve minimum fabrication, best suited to services and structure in discrete zones with limited overlap.

- ↘ Fabricated sections
  Optimum material content, but require greater workmanship – provide 'shaping' to facilitate overlap between services and structure. Can lend itself to automated fabrication.

Good arrangements are often a selected mix of these options.

- ↘ Concrete slabs
  Ribbed slabs on spine beams, shaped to save weight and multiple re-use of formwork – rectangular grids encourage uniform soffit levels.

- ↘ Flat slabs
  Shaped to simplify fast, repetitive shuttering and helped by post-tensioning, but heavier than steel/metal deck options.

Steel and concrete composite floor system:
Rolled sections:
30 St Mary Axe, London, Foster and Partners.
↓   © Arup

Steel and concrete composite floor system:
Fabricated sections:
Commerzbank HQ Frankfurt, Germany, Foster and Partners.
↓↓   © Arup

Steel and concrete composite floor system:
Automatic cellular beams:
More London, London, Foster and Partners.
↓   © Arup

Concrete may offer the lowest structural floor thickness, but prevents overlap of spaces for the structure and the services – the overall floor depth for 'structure and services' may be higher.

Mixed use buildings require careful consideration, as the most commonly adopted systems for offices and residential purposes differ. As buildings get taller, the need to achieve a fast, repetitive system for the overall economies of the venture becomes an important driver. In either material, rectangular grids, with the longer spans spanning frequently, and the shorter spans carrying the heavy reactions, lead to economy and consistency of depth. Tall buildings may well have longer span floors, and checks of their vibration characteristics should be carried out to ensure occupancy comfort. Edge beams should adopt stiffnesses that are co-ordinated with the capability of perimeter cladding to take movement.

Robustness

The UK building codes have guidance that provides a measure of robustness against the potential for progressive collapse. These provisions would be incorporated in designs as a matter of course. They are likely to cope with a serious event, but may be overcome by a drastic extreme event. Industry deliberations are in hand on the case for more particular provisions. Should clients feel that their facilities may require a strategically enhanced approach, there are options to consider. A broader risk assessment based approach may then be appropriate.

Concrete floors:
Ribbed slab:
88 Wood Street, London, Richard Rogers Partnership.
↓   © Arup

Concrete floors:
Ribbed slab with post-tensioning:
88 Wood Street, London, Richard Rogers Partnership.
↓↓   © Arup

Concrete floors:
Flat slab:
Chiswick Park, London, Richard Rogers Partnership.
↓   © Arup/David J Osborn

Tolerances and movement

Structures are constructed to a tolerance which departs from a theoretically perfect shape. This results in all parts of the structure being 'out of true', but preferably within specified limits. Tall buildings tend to have greater tolerances than those of lower height. As a result, building components which are to be 'true' in their finished state need to be allocated the space to accommodate variations in the structural position. Examples are lift shafts and cladding.

Structures move as they accommodate loads. Vertical loads result in beams deflecting and columns shortening. Lateral loads lead to frames swaying, imposing a horizontal movement between one floor and another below.

These movements need to be kept within appropriate limits, and more crucially, the finishing elements such as cladding, lift shaft lining, lift guide rails should be designed for compatible movements with one another and the structure. It can be more expensive to make provision for high flexibility in finishing elements than it is to limit movements in the structure, either by material or choice of structural form. A 'tolerance and movement' report is recommended as an early project standard.

Occupancy comfort

Tall buildings are susceptible to oscillation caused by the action of wind. The lateral oscillation can often be felt by occupants in strong winds, and is therefore an issue for the comfort of building users.

Acceptance criteria have been developed by surveying people who live and work in tall buildings, relating to the peak level of acceleration likely to be experienced within a certain period. The acceptability of the predicted acceleration is a function of both 'perception' (what people feel) and 'acceptability' (some people will feel more acceleration than others, but may also be more tolerant of it). With mixed use, the criteria for comfort are more stringent for residential units, particularly if the building is tall and slender.

Where dampers are considered, they may take an active or passive form, and work on the principle of building movements dissipating energy into carefully 'tuned suspended masses', mounted in a tall building's upper levels. Consideration needs to be given to the building performance in the event of a damping system shutting down.

↘ A 'tolerance and movement' report is recommended as an early project standard.

Tolerance and movement:
30 St Mary Axe, London, Foster and Partners.
→   © David Hawkins Ibipp

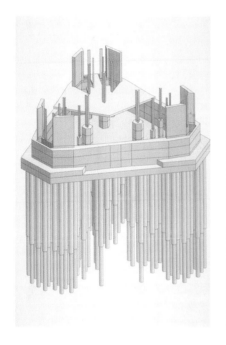

↑ Commerzbank HQ Frankfurt, Germany:
   The dense clusters of piles below the perimeter
   cores reflect the intensity of load concentrations at
   these points.
   © Arup

↑ Commerzbank HQ Frankfurt, Germany:
   Large diameter bored piling under construction.
   © Arup

Substructure and foundations

Basements and foundations take significant time to construct. A vital aspect of the economics of tall buildings is the period over which financing has to be 'carried' before it earns a return. An opposing pressure is for good use to be made of high value land. To balance this equation effectively, the size and complexity of substructures should be carefully considered. For example, some historic and recent tall buildings in London have no basements under the footprint, while others have been developed with as many as three.

Tall buildings produce high loads in concentrated locations. This calls for high capacity foundations, with manageable settlement characteristics. The type of foundations needed reflect the area's geology. For example:

⬂ New York:
   Rock at shallow depth

⬂ Hong Kong and Singapore:
   Rock at medium depths

⬂ London:
   London clay for considerable depths, overlying sands and chalk.

Where the geology is inherently firm, tall buildings may have straightforward foundations, while more flexible ground strata need more considered foundation designs and analytical/movement prediction techniques. Good geotechnical engineering will help to optimise this unseen aspect of tall buildings.

Cities like London have a long history of using underground tunnels for transport, communications and services. Searches are required to establish their presence and their form of construction, and where appropriate, to develop the substructure and foundation techniques to safeguard these. Historic and future infrastructure can significantly influence the 'site footprints' that can be relied on, and how they may be developed.

↑   Central Plaza, Hong Kong:
Tall buildings in Hong Kong frequently employ large
diameter caissons for their foundations. This reflects
local building skills and geotechnical ground
conditions.
© Arup

↑   30 St Mary Axe, London:
Construction sequences for tall buildings are
necessarily overlapped to minimise overall
construction periods. This shows the simultaneous
construction of frame, flooring, fire-proofing and
cladding at different heights in the building.
© David Hawkins Ibipp

↑   Principality Building Society HQ, Cardiff:
An example of 'top down' basement construction
which allows basement works below to occur
concurrently with superstructure works above,
optimising project programme.
© STP Photography

Construction

In addition to providing a building's skeleton
which can inform its character, the structural
form needs to be effective and manageable to
build, and facilitate achievement of the project
business case. Given that construction time
increases as buildings become taller, realism is
needed on the time they may take to build, and
the characteristics which most influence this.

Each aspect of tall building structures should
therefore be optimised for material content,
cost and time. The main structural drivers in
this are the choices for the structural form,
floor system and substructure/foundations.
The balance between repetition and variety
in the structure can be vital. Constrained
inner city sites entail particular logistical
issues to overcome.

Fred Pilbrow
KPF

The envelope

The envelope design for a tall building will be informed by the building's required aesthetic appearance, technical performance, the approach to its construction and its future maintenance. These objectives relate to both building's exterior and interior. Accordingly, the design will be developed with the input and collaboration of a range of specialists.

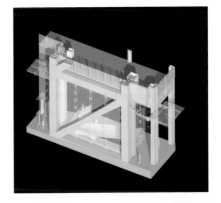

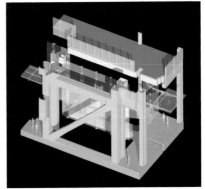

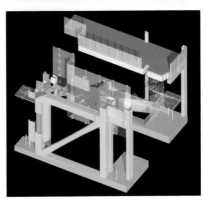

Heron Tower, 110 Bishopsgate
KPF, consented 2002

→   Detail of north elevation describing the layering of the structure.
© Hayes Davidson/KPF

←   View from Bishopsgate: the building's elevation is enriched by both its structural system and internal arrangement. On the north elevation, the braced expression of the perimeter structural tube underscores the three-storey arrangement of office 'villages', with the atrium at the centre of each village legible on the elevation.
© Hayes Davidson

Appearance

The external appearance of a tall builing will be determined by the proportions and interrelationship of its façades and roof, including any roof-top enclosures and structures. Some of these elements, like the façade, will also inform the building's internal character.

Views

The appearance is the outcome of both the building's massing and its elevational treatment. In long-distance views, the overall form of the building is most critical to its appearance. As one approaches the building, the modelling of the façade and its fenestration become more dominant, and viewed close by, the façade materials and details come into focus.

Façade

The elevation affords an opportunity to express the building's internal organisation, imparting external legibility to its internal functions. The façade may also be informed by the building's structural and servicing systems. The choice of structural stablity system is an example of this. Central core stability strategies free the perimeter from a primary structural role, allowing an open expression to the façade. Conversely, a perimeter stability tube will place considerable structure at the façade. This need not be negative. For example, Swiss Re's diagonal perimeter tube informs and enriches the character of its façade. The overall form can be an important generator for the elevation, emphasising the character of the structure. Swiss Re provides an example of this too, with the arrangement of the triangular panels responding to the geometry of the building, allowing flat glazed panels to follow its external form. The design of the façade should respond to orientation and aspect. This is likely to inform its appearance. The townscape setting and the building's relationship to key prospects should also influence the treatment of the façade.

Exterior palette

Façade materials range from the highly transparent, through translucent, to opaque. They can be varied in colour and texture, lending the elevation visual weight or lightness.

Grain

The façade will be assembled from a number of repetitive components which generate pattern and grain.

Hierarchy

Because of their size, tall buildings are seen in distant, mid- and local views. An elevation composed with elements of varied weight and scale can establish a hierarchy that reads legibly in the respective views.

Detail

As the building is approached, new levels of detail should resolve themselves so that the façade maintains its visual richness. At the closest range, the tactile quality of the façade materials becomes important.

↑→ De Hoftoren, The Hague, KPF, completed 2003.
© H.G Esch

Layering and depth

Façades which incorporate a high degree of transparency offer scope to develop layering and depth. This allows elements of structure and circulation to participate in the visual richness of the façade.

Scale

Detail at the base of the building should be of finer scale than the detailing at its top, as the latter is seen only at some distance.

Day and night

Tall buildings are especially prominent at night. The interplay of light, structure and enclosure can underpin the legibility of the building's organisation.

Internal appearance

The character of the façade can support the connection between the building's interior and exterior. The façade should maximise the potential for views from and daylight in the building, whilst providing an appropriate degree of privacy and feeling of safety. The treatment of the internal face of the façade should avoid a dark and flat reflective appearance at night. The internal space planning considerations will inform the grain of the façade which will be planned to allow for flexibility in office partitioning.

↗→ De Hoftoren frames a new public garden court and opens new routes across the site. The visual density of the building's elevations responds to orientation and aspect. The elevation is more opaque to the south and more open to the garden. Each façade is conceived as a plane. Reveals at the corners provide visual separation between adjacent elevations.
© H.G Esch

Performance

The envelope functions as an environmental modifier. It ameliorates or enhances the effects of the external environment to create an interior that is dry, at a comfortable temperature, sufficiently daylit without glare, as well as pleasant acoustically.

These internal environmental conditions are achieved through the envelope and the building services systems. The aim is for the envelope to achieve most of the performance requirements, thereby minimising energy usage associated with the building servicing. The envelope and the services design are therefore developed in a co-ordinated way. Efficiencies in the envelope's performance will allow savings in the capital cost of servicing plant, as well as savings in future costs to run the building.

Ventilation

The building may be naturally ventilated, air-conditioned, or offer a combination of these modes. In a naturally ventilated building, the façade will be detailed to deal with the high wind pressures associated with tall buildings. Whilst there is cost and complexity associated with this provision, the opportunity to ventilate the building naturally can offer energy and comfort benefits.

Weather tightness

The envelope needs to address the issues of condensation, water penetration and air infiltration.

Thermal moderation

The envelope will need to control heat loss and heat gain. Recent developments in active, ventilated façades have sought to marry visual transparency with high thermal performance. Such façades can respond to diurnal and seasonal changes

Comfort

The comfort needs of occupants will also inform the façade design. People are sensitive to the radiant sun's heat and draughts.

Light

Whilst it is appropriate to maximise the available daylight to the building interior, the façade must ensure that a balance is struck to prevent glare. Further, highly reflective elements in the façade can create problems of intensive glare for neighbouring buildings.

Acoustics

The façade must provide appropriate acoustic isolation of the interior to limit disturbance from external noise. It can also contribute to an appropriate internal acoustic environnment by controlling reverberation time. Where necessary, the façade can also prevent noise break-out from plant, vehicles and other sources.

Kuwait Business City, KPF, design development 2005

The south elevation of the tall office building is curved in plan and section. A hanging veil of fritted glass shades protect the interior from solar gain. A proportion of these shades are coloured on the building's exterior (the internal frit is neutral in tone). The distribution of these coloured panels emphasises the geometrical form of the building.

↓↓ South façade, detail plan.
     © KPF

↓   South façade, detail elevation.
     © KPF

↓   South façade, detail section.
     © KPF

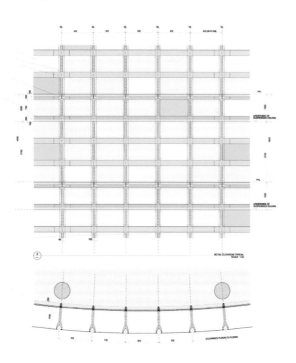

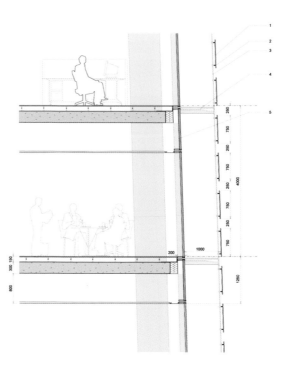

Wind loading

Whilst the British Standards give guidance on calculating wind loadings of tall buildings, wind tunnel testing is beneficial expose local areas of the building where the form generates higher loads, testing will allow the design of the façade to be optimised.

Fire

The envelope will be designed to reflect fire and life safety considerations. The façade will control fire spread between buildings and compartments. Openable areas will provide for smoke ventilation provided this does not compromise the safety.

Security

The façade can be designed for enhanced security and blast resistance. In designing for blast, consideration will be given both to the safety of the building's occupants and the potential impact that falling debris might have on people outside the building.

→   Kuwait Business City, exterior view.
     © Hayes Davidson
↓   Detail of fritted glass screen.
     © Hayes Davidson

Construction and maintenance

The form of construction adopted for a tall building's façade and the strategy for its maintenance and potential replacement will also inform its design. Façades can be load bearing or non-load bearing. The latter can be designed within the structural frame or as a 'curtain wall' outside the line of the structure.

Cladding approaches and systems
Façades can be built entirely on site, for example, where masonry is laid by hand. More commonly, pre-fabrication is preferred because it offers the potential for reduced construction time and simpler logistics.

Adia, Abu Dhabi, KPF, under construction 2005
←   © Eamonn O'Mahony
↓   © KPF

Pre-fabricated cladding can entail:

- Unitised cladding
- Panelised cladding

The construction method to be adopted is usually informed by a range of factors including: appearance, performance, cost, construction programme, safe methods of access and handling and long term maintenance.

Buildability

Installing cladding on a tall building site is usually challenging. Inner city sites in the UK are often small, with limited space for delivery and storage. Cladding will be programmed to overlap with the completion of the super-structure, which requires close co-ordination where there are shared access systems. Delivering the cladding to the point of installation involves long, vertical travel distances. The high wind speeds at the top of tall buildings add to the difficulties.

In response to these challenges, cladding will usually be pre-fabricated. Choosing a unitised cladding system will allow units to be installed from the floors of the building, rather than from a crane. This has the advantages of being less wind sensitive, and allows the panels to be stored locally before being installed.

During the design phase, a cleaning and maintenance regime will be worked out with the input of specialists. Dedicated access equipment will be provided. The location of cradles and their restraint in use will inform the cladding design.

The maintenance strategy is likely to maximise the amount of work that can be done from the floor itself, or through use of the building's own access equipment. Long term maintenance access can be provided by permanent or temporary rigs on the building or mobile crane access from the street. Cleaning

and maintenance regimes will also need to be designed for internal atria, glazed lift shafts and stairs.

Façade replacement

As well as providing for cleaning access, the façade will be designed to allow for glass or panel replacement in the event of accidental damage or the failure of double-glazed units. Gaskets and sealants will need to be replaced and elements of the façade may require re-finishing.

Tolerance and movement

There will be a balance to be struck between the stiffness of the structural frame and the capacity of the cladding to accept movement. The more the cladding needs to accept movement, the wider the joints needed. Smaller cladding modules allow such movement tolerance to be distributed across more panels, with narrower joints.

←← Two curved wings flank an atrium that rises up the full height of the building. The atrium, oriented to the north west to overlook the Gulf, is protected from solar gain by the building's mass. The other building elevations are triple-glazed, ventilated façades that combine transparency with excellent thermal peformance.
© KPF

← The fine vertical grain of the elevations facilitate the building's sinuous plan form, without the necessity of curved glass.
© KPF

The future

Likely future regulation will require higher performance from buildings, including greater energy efficiency. The static 'best fit' approach to façade design falls short of the optimum performance that could be attained relative to changing climatic conditions outside buildings. Dynamic façades that are able to respond to such changes may therefore become commonplace.

Through their incorporation of innovations, tall buildings are contributing to the development of cost-effective solutions in the field. Such projects both fund research and provide support for a critical size of market to support cost effective production.

The potential for renewable energy generation in tall buildings is considerable. For example, the high wind speeds at the top of tall buildings have the potential to generate wind power. Recent projects in London, like the Heron Tower, have integrated photovoltaic panels and wind turbines on south facing elevations.

Automated cleaning systems are being installed on buildings in the Far East and manufacturers are now marketing self-cleaning glass.

> ↘ Likely future regulation will require higher performance from buildings, including greater energy efficiency. The static 'best fit' approach to façade design falls short of the optimum performance that could be attained relative to changing climatic conditions outside buildings..

↙↓ Heron Tower, KPF, consented 2002
Detail of south elevation 'active wall' incorporating photovoltaics and wind turbines.
© Foreman Roberts

→ The Mori Tower, Shanghai, KPF,
under construction 2005. Buildings in the Far East are far taller than any that are considered appropriate for the UK. Nevertheless, their design innovation often produces technological developments that are relevant and beneficial to the UK context. The building pioneers robotic cleaning.
© KPF

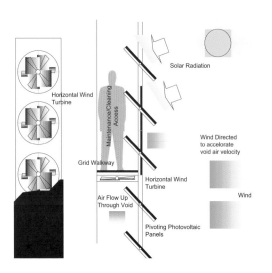

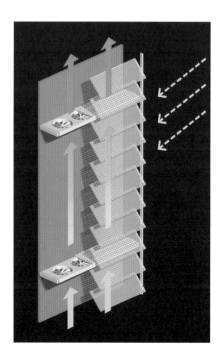

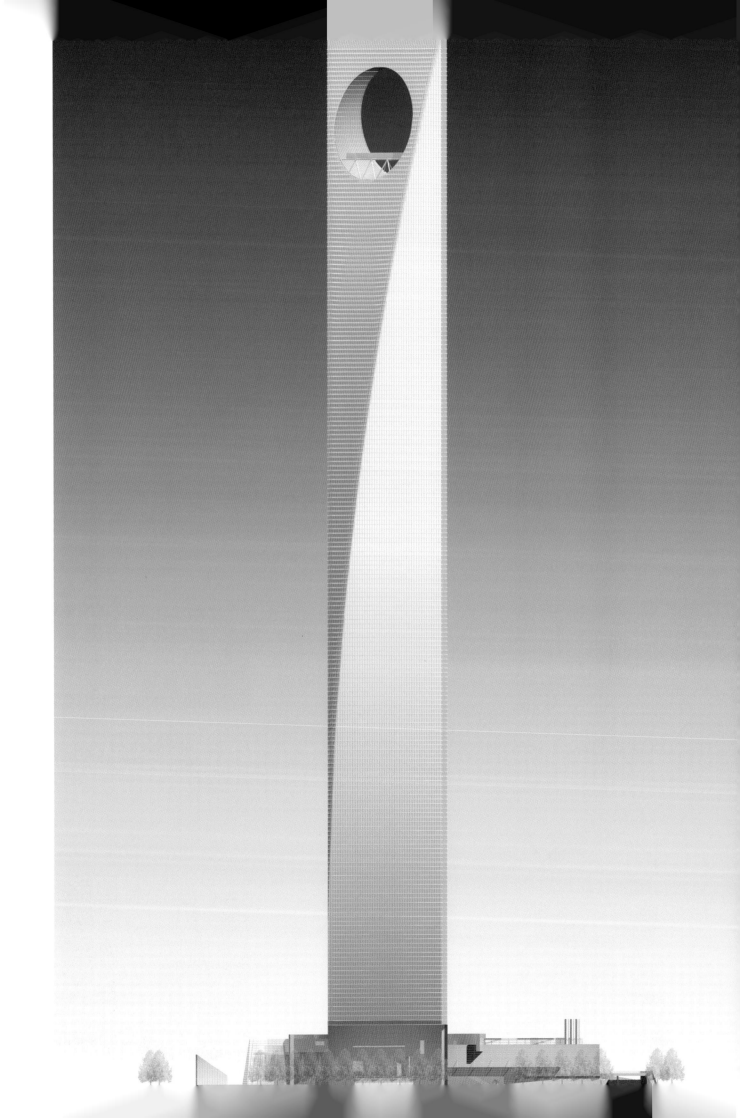

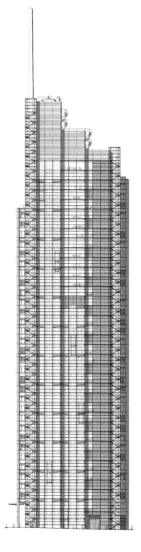

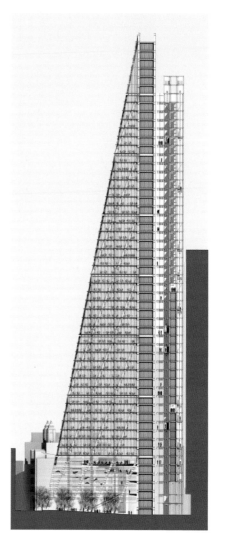

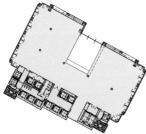

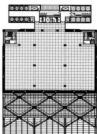

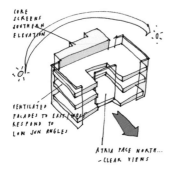

Heron Tower, 110 Bishopsgate,
KPF, consented 2002

The building's form underpins its environmental
strategy. A south facing core protects the office
interior from solar gain. A north facing atrium
provides even daylight to the workplace.
←↖ © KPF

122 Leadenhall Street, Richard Rogers Partnership,
consented 2004

A series of externally ventilated 7 storey high façade
modules protects the south facing offices from
external solar gains.
↗→ © Richard Rogers Partnership

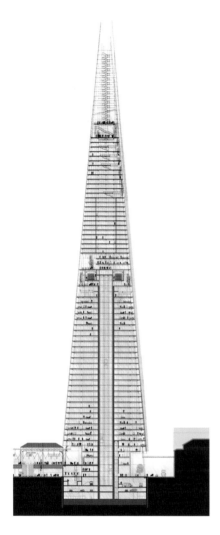

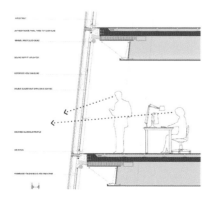

Mohsen Zikri
Arup

Services
Building form and façade

Optimising the building form, orientation and thermal characteristics of the façade has a direct impact on space for plant and risers, the building's energy consumption and its future maintenance costs. The design of these elements is achieved by an iterative process. To yield meaningful benefits for the building's future performance, this must occur in the conceptual phase of the building design, in close collaboration by the architectural and structural teams and other specialists involved. This process should recognise the specific architectural concept of the building.

The building's plan, volumetric form and orientation should be analysed with the aim of reducing heating and cooling loads, whilst optimising daylight. Part L of the Building Regulations dictates the minimum benchmark for energy use. Contemporary best practice would apply passive methods to minimise energy use as a primary objective. For example, locating cores externally on the south and west orientation reduces thermal loads, provided this arrangement is feasible and acceptable architecturally.

London Bridge Tower, Renzo Piano Building Workshop, consented 2003.

Individual building elevations respond to their specific orientation through a range of shading configurations.
← © Renzo Piano Building Workshop

Energy issues

The focus on energy is accentuated by the requirements of tall buildings' vertical circulation and the inherent magnitude of their external surfaces. Typically, 60-70% of the total energy used in a building is accounted for by the façade. Design approaches to mitigate this include minimising the façade area by optimising storey height, and specifying façades with superior environmental performance.

Where tall buildings can be naturally ventilated in parts in the appropriate periods of spring and autumn, this will save energy in use. However, as the plant and equipment to cater for peak winter and summer conditions will still be required, 'mixed mode' ventilated buildings will not be less expensive in terms of their capital cost.

The use of BREEAM (Building Research Establishment's Environmental Assessment Method) as an environmental assessment framework is the current UK industry standard. Whilst its use is mostly elective, some planning authorities have made it mandatory for planning proposals to demonstrate that designs meet these criteria.

The BREEAM framework does not include a specific focus on the energy required by lift use, though this contributes to the overall energy required to run the building. The use of double-deck lifts is primarily aimed at reducing core areas, rather than energy use. Advances in lift drives and control technologies help to a degree, although they seldom result in a quantum leap in energy savings. The energy consumed by vertical travel within the building should be balanced against the reduced energy on travel to the building, if the tall building is appropriately sited close to transport nodes, and if users' actual travel modes reflect this condition.

↘ The scale of a tall building increases the importance of exploiting natural energy sources and using renewable energy. This is relevant for social and environmental costs as well as for costs in use.

The scale of a tall building increases the importance of exploiting natural energy sources and using renewable energy. This is relevant for social and environmental costs as well as for costs in use. Embodied energy also affects a building's thermal properties. For example, a 'heavy' concrete construction enhances the beneficial effect of the building's thermal inertia. However, producing concrete in the first place is an energy intensive process. On the other hand, a steel construction offers less thermal inertia and involves lower embodied energy, but lends itself to recycling and speed of construction. These are examples of design considerations and trade-offs that need to be integrated. All design strategies will need to be reconciled with the ease and speed of construction which affect the project's outturn cost.

Infiltration and air tightness

The significant wind pressures to which a tall building is subjected accentuate the importance of controlling air leakage through the façade. Air infiltration has a direct impact on the energy required to heat and cool the building. The façade design should recognise this and appropriate tests should be undertaken at the earliest possible stage of the design (refer to BSRIA – Building Services Research and Information Associates – Part L document).

Design and procurement: summary of criteria.
The illustration shows the predicited BREEAM rating for the London Bridge Tower.
© KPF/Arup

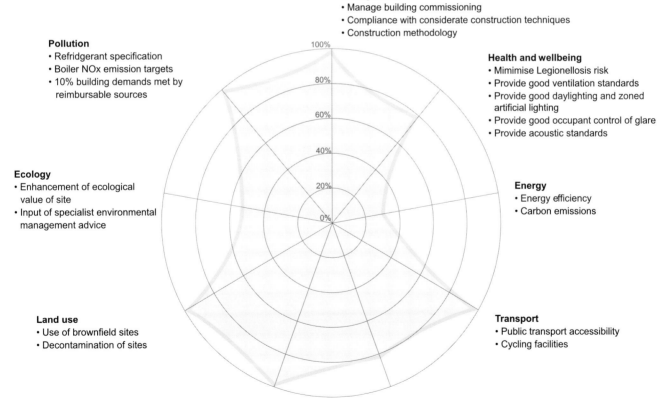

Management
• Manage building commissioning
• Compliance with considerate construction techniques
• Construction methodology

Pollution
• Refridgerant specification
• Boiler NOx emission targets
• 10% building demands met by reimbursable sources

Health and wellbeing
• Mimimise Legionellosis risk
• Provide good ventilation standards
• Provide good daylighting and zoned artificial lighting
• Provide good occupant control of glare
• Provide acoustic standards

Ecology
• Enhancement of ecological value of site
• Input of specialist environmental management advice

Energy
• Energy efficiency
• Carbon emissions

Land use
• Use of brownfield sites
• Decontamination of sites

Transport
• Public transport accessibility
• Cycling facilities

Materials
• Building materials evaluated with ENVEST*
• Recycling facilities
• Sustainable sourced materials

Water consumption
• Predicted level of water consumption
• Metering
• Leak detection

*Software tool to design building with lower environmental impact and whole life costs.

Mechanical services

The choice of air-conditioning system, through its impact on the core size and the building's floor-to-floor height, has significant implications for space efficiency and internal environmental quality. In the case of comfort cooling installations, water-based systems such as fan coil units are more space-efficient when compared with all air systems, such as VAV. Mechanical services risers should be designed to accommodate movements generated not only by vertical expansion and contraction, but also from the horizontal sway of the building as a result of wind pressures.

Underfloor air supply with chilled ceiling

↓   © Arup/KPF

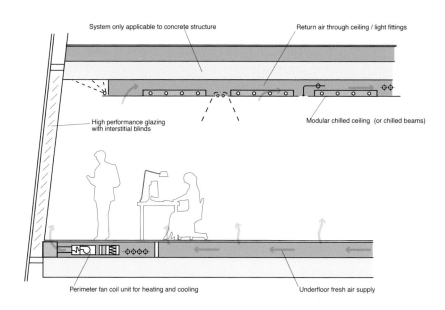

System only applicable to concrete structure

Return air through ceiling / light fittings

High performance glazing with interstitial blinds

Modular chilled ceiling (or chilled beams)

Perimeter fan coil unit for heating and cooling

Underfloor fresh air supply

**Air handling units and
intermediate electrical transformers:
Strategic options for tall buildings**

↓   © Arup/KPF

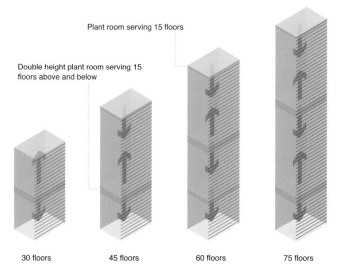

Plant room serving 15 floors

Double height plant room serving 15 floors above and below

| 30 floors | 45 floors | 60 floors | 75 floors |

Commercial and planning pressures dictate the need to optimise floor-to-ceiling heights. The horizontal integration of the mechanical services with the building structure may yield savings in storey height, but this needs careful examination to ensure that it does not compromise any structural or mechanical elements, including requirements for maintenance access and equipment replacement.

Air-handling plant needs to be distributed in dedicated plant rooms across the height of the building. The number of floors served by each air plant is influenced by the type of air-conditioning system that is adopted, e.g. an all-air system versus water-based with minimum fresh air.

Air intake and exhaust serving all ventilation plants should be carefully designed and positioned to ensure that wind pressures on the building façade do not adversely affect the function of air intake and exhaust openings. Heating and cooling plants are normally centralised to achieve efficiencies through load diversification. Structural considerations favour placing heavy equipment at lower levels, typically in basements if this is viable.

Static water pressures are an issue in the case of water systems. It is essential to deal with the build-up of static water pressures that is applied to pipe work fittings and the equipment served. Distributing water tanks across the height of the building in dedicated plant rooms may be used as a part of a zoning strategy to limit static pressures.

The main external infrastructure should cater for alternative providers of services. Intake rooms should be easily accessible and well protected for safety and security reasons. The use of broadband and fibre optic cables should be recognised during the early design stages.

Electrical services

The inherent vertical configuration for this type of building makes it appropriate to distribute high and low voltage equipment in intermediate plant rooms across the height of the building. Design and cost considerations determine the maximum number of floors served by one plant room. Vertical cabling should allow for building sway from wind-generated movement.

Electrical standby generation

Stand-by provisions are critical for the base building, as they have to support life safety systems. Support for power failure is less onerous, with the extent of cover normally dictated by commercial and business needs.

Multi-tenancy and mixed use situations require additional facilities for electrical stand-by generation. These requirements differ from project to project, but must be recognised at an early stage of the design.

Strategic options for water systems

↓   © KPF/Arup

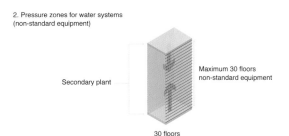

1. Pressure zones for water systems (standard equipment)

Pressure zone (maximum 15 floors)

Pressure zone

Pressure zone

Secondary plant

Pressure zone

60 floors

2. Pressure zones for water systems (non-standard equipment)

Secondary plant

Maximum 30 floors non-standard equipment

30 floors

Stand-by generation: (base build)

↓   © KPF/Arup

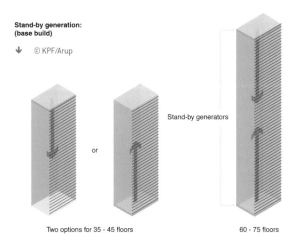

Stand-by generators

or

Two options for 35 - 45 floors

60 - 75 floors

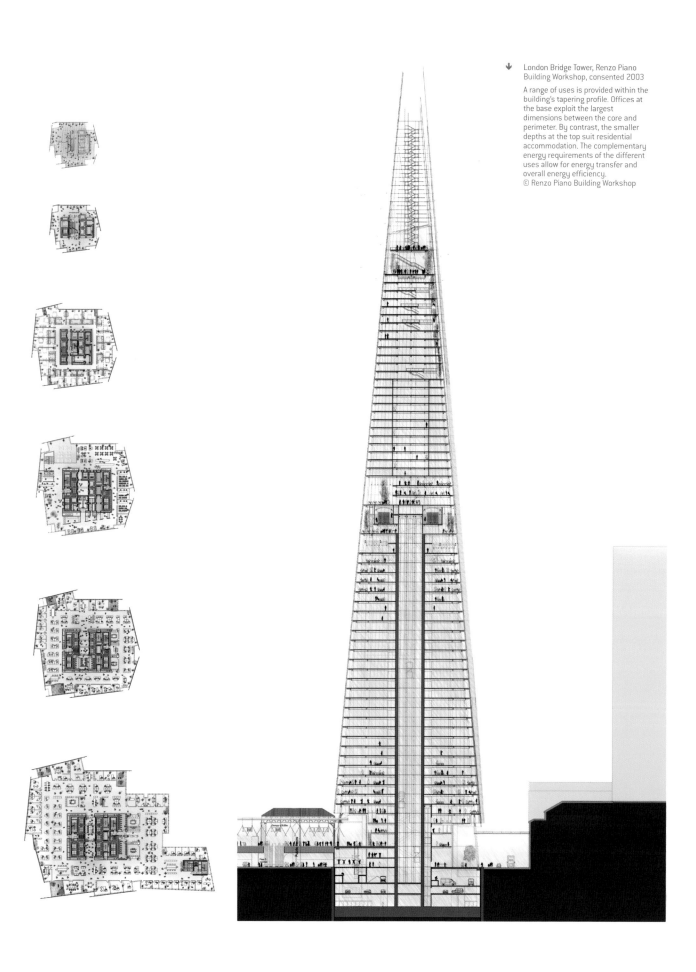

↓   London Bridge Tower, Renzo Piano
Building Workshop, consented 2003

A range of uses is provided within the
building's tapering profile. Offices at
the base exploit the largest
dimensions between the core and
perimeter. By contrast, the smaller
depths at the top suit residential
accommodation. The complementary
energy requirements of the different
uses allow for energy transfer and
overall energy efficiency.
© Renzo Piano Building Workshop

Providing for mixed use

In mixed use tall buildings, there is typically a need for independent mechanical plant and risers for each type of use. As this increases the core size considerably, its impact should be considered at a very early stage of the design.

Mixed use tall buildings also involve the provision of independent electrical plant and systems. The extent differs with the types of use and occupier profiles.

IT and data

The vertical configuration of tall buildings favours decentralised systems of equipment. This may also satisfy security aspects, as well as catering for multi-tenancy.

Life cycle costing

This is an increasingly important aspect which generally requires added investment at the outset to achieve lower costs in use.

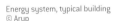

Energy system, typical building
↓   © Arup

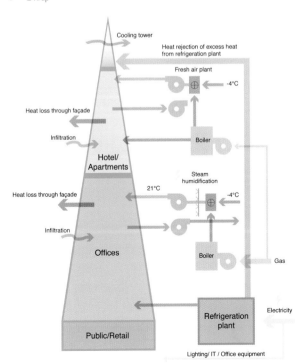

London Bridge Tower, proposed system
↓   © Arup

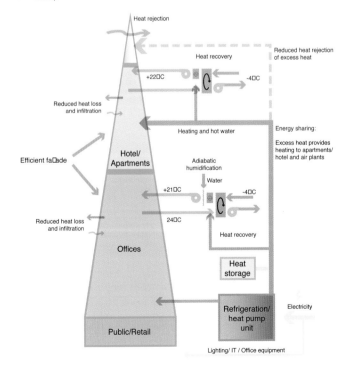

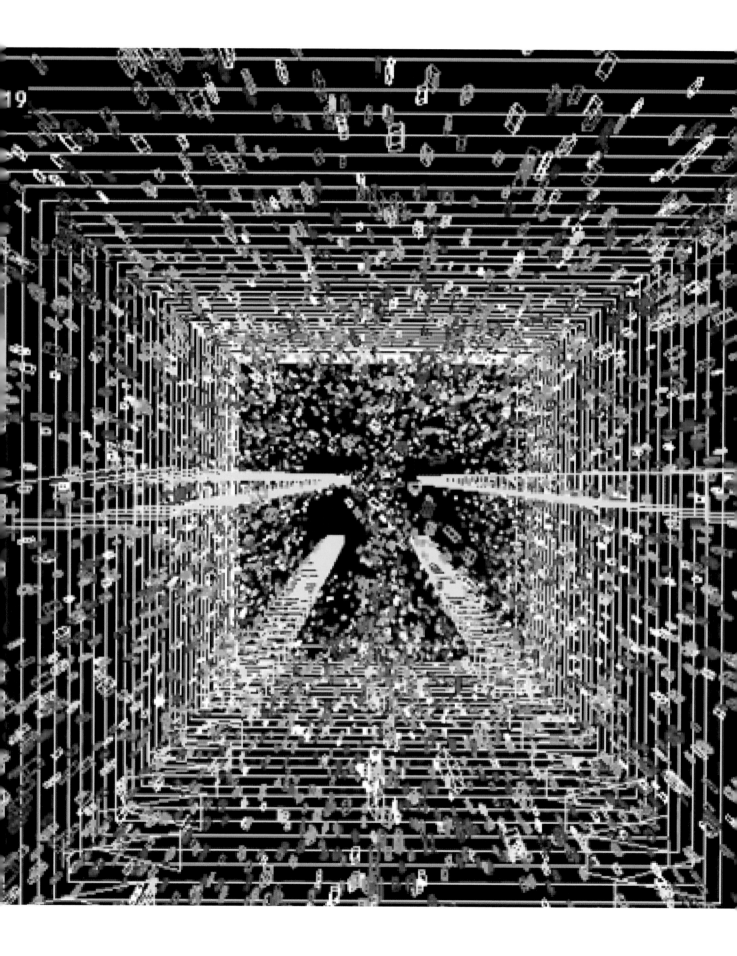

19

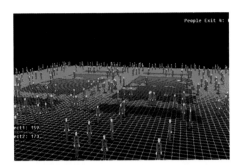

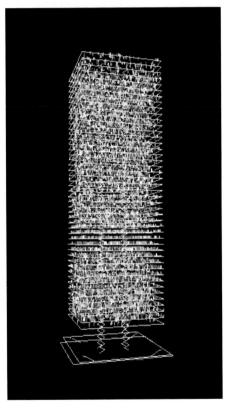

Faith Wainwright
Arup

Safety
Life safety strategies

Protection of occupants in tall buildings in the event of an accident that damages the building is achieved principally through structural robustness and fire safety measures. Of fundamental importance is the need to evacuate the building safely. Prior to 11 September 2001, fire procedures in tall buildings involved evacuating the fire floor and the floor above, with staged alarms in other parts of larger buildings if the fire incident was not terminated. Recently, events have led owners to provide for evacuation of the whole building at once, although this approach is currently elective. This challenging objective requires consideration of the capacity and robustness of the exit routes, the use of lifts as well as stairs, the organisation of emergency response plans and training of building managers and occupants.

Lifts can be used to evacuate occupants if there is warning of an imminent event. Potentially, lifts could also be used when a fire or blast has damaged the building. This approach is still being explored at a research level. It would require robustness of the lift shaft construction, protection against fire and smoke, and back-up and continuity of electrical supplies to be considered in the design. Using lifts for evacuation can have benefits, as lifts have been shown to halve the evacuation time for a building of around 40 storeys.

In 'whole building evacuation' studies, the design process involves consideration of different scenarios, e.g. an escape staircase being out of action, and then evaluating the benefit of increasing stair/lift evacuation capacity. The comfort of occupants during evacuation may be improved by organising refuge spaces from which final evacuation by lift may be possible. This has an impact on the design and maintenance of stand-by electrical facilities, as well as on space planning.

←↑ Evacuation time can be predicted with analytical modelling tools.
© Arup

Basic precautions against an attack involving biological or chemical agents include location of air intakes in places where public access is difficult, and incorporating security into plant room access. More specialised measures, such as adopting separate HVAC zones or incorporating high efficiency particulate air (HEPA) filters, can be taken if deemed appropriate following risk assessment studies.

Apart from the need to assure occupants that safety measures will protect them, disruption to business from a damaging event can be significant. The potential benefits of enhanced life-safety measures, over and above the mandatory fire life-safety provisions outlined below, warrant careful assessment.

Fire life safety

The evolving practice such as outlined above is in addition to the mandatory provision for life safety required by Building Regulations. Meeting the latter nevertheless requires co-ordinated design effort to integrate the provisions with optimal design, in particular, to achieve means of escape and fire brigade access. The key issues are control of fire, management of escape and speed of fire brigade access and set-up.

Strategies embodied in the Building Regulations requirements are the use of

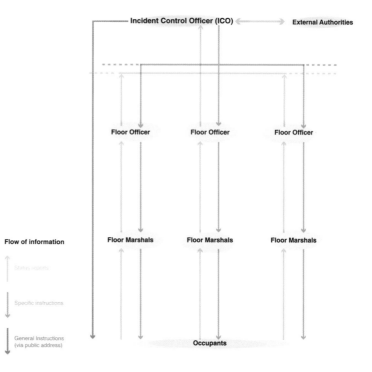

→ The design of a robust security strategy for a tall
   building proposal will be based on a thorough risk
   assessment. The evaluation of risk and the
   development of design responses to mitigate these
   risks is an iterative process.
   © Arup

→ Accurate information is necessary for determining
   the appropriate response. This requires an effective
   chain of communication for emergencies.
   © Arup

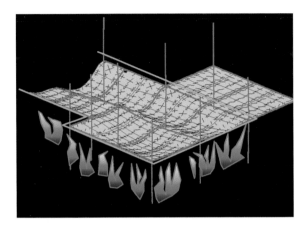

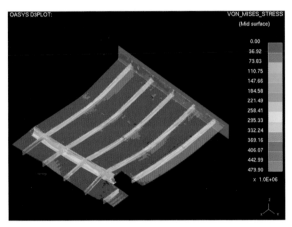

Finite element analysis of floors allows the response of the structure in fire conditions to be predicted.
← ↖ © Arup

The International Finance Centre in Hong Kong was under construction when the World Trade Centre was attacked in New York. The design was assesed for new damage scenarios with advanced modelling techniques.
← © Arup

automatic suppression, phasing or staging of evacuation, and the use of lifts for the fire brigade in protected and ventilated stairs. The main fire life safety features for a tall building are:

- Floor-by-floor compartmentation with protection of shafts that link floors

- Escape stairs arranged so that there is at least one within a short distance of every point on every floor and that there are enough alternative exits to stairs

- Automatic smoke control systems

- Fire brigade access via lifts in well protected 'firefighting shafts', including stairs and lobbies with special protection against smoke and fire

- Wayfinding signage and escape lighting with secondary power.

Additional features that may be used to enhance life safety provision may include provisions for communicating to building users, e.g. dedicated CCTV and PA systems in staircases.

Modelling

Determining value from a range of potential life-safety measures should begin with assessing the client's objectives and an assessment of risk. A wide range of scenarios and mitigation measures can then be considered before evaluating which measures yield the greatest benefit.

Simulation of scenarios using evacuation modelling, structural finite element modelling and computational fluid dynamics to consider how the structure will perform in a fire or other damage events are valuable tools in undertaking these assessments. They allow design to be 'performance-based', i.e. to be based on the real behaviour of the building, rather than being based on a codified set of rules. Using performance-based design, it is often possible to improve performance without increased cost, or to realise design ambitions such as incorporating large open multi-storey spaces which would otherwise be unacceptable under the Building Regulations.

cost:

↘ The cost and scarcity of developable land, the permitted footprint, building bulk, quality of specification, and the time required for design, construction, occupation and use are all generic cost drivers of buildings. The cost of any particular mix of these influences the economics of a building – whether short, tall, large or small.

STEVE WATTS DAVIS LANGDON

Optimal design solutions can identify 'appropriate cost'. When factored into a building's performance, this can have a measurable influence on the productivity of the spaces enclosed. It may or may not support the initial cost of a building (as space from which to transact business) over its operational life cycle. The creation of a landmark is a related issue.

Procuring tall buildings

The size, complexity and duration of tall building projects means that there are a limited number of ways to design and construct them, in terms of both strategy and the range of designers, contractors and specialists with the skills, experience and resources to undertake the work. This section considers key issues in developing a successful procurement strategy for tall buildings.

← Tall buildings in the City of London.
The historic street pattern of the City of London creates small, often complex footprints. The proximity of listed buildings and conservation areas influences the modelling and articulation of tall buildings. Both factors serve to produce structures of relatively high cost.
© Hayes Davidson

Speed and efficiency

One of the main opportunities of tall building design and construction is the ability to exploit the benefits of standardisation and repetition across major cost elements, such as the façades. The scale of tall buildings makes this true even when a building is bespoke. Achieving and maintaining speed is critical to successful project delivery. Procurement strategies that allow the overlapping of design, procurement and construction are essential to achieve acceptable project durations.

To optimise the programme and eliminate potential sources of delay and disruption, it is vital to invest in strategic construction planning and buildability reviews at an early stage. Key elements in programming tall building projects include:

⬂ Management and co-ordination of trade activities on site, to maintain the cycle of floor construction

⬂ Management of extended design and procurement programmes, to permit the maximum degree of standardisation and minimise floor construction cycles

⬂ Optimising the use of standardised and pre-fabricated components and other measures to promote 'buildability'.

Specialist contractors

The procurement of specialist contractors is strongly influenced by the size of packages involved. It can be beneficial to bundle related trades into a single package with united management. Examples of this are core area fit-out works and services installations. The early appointment of specialist contractors is essential to provide for their early design input and co-ordination. For example, a concrete trade contractor may influence the choice of core construction method, which could result in changes to its design.

Logistics

Provision of sufficient cranage and hoisting is critical to maintain programme. Co-ordination of deliveries, cranage slots and construction programmes is necessary to ensure that speed is maintained. Efficient transport of people and materials is crucial to achieve productive utilisation of labour. On tall structures, the added time taken to travel to and from higher level workfaces calls for attention to vertical transport during the construction period and provision for worker welfare above ground level. The location of toilets and canteens at regular intervals up the building will minimise downtime and prevent delays through unnecessary journeys in hoists.

Health and safety

Health and safety is a major issue when working at height. The attention paid to these requirements during tall building construction in the UK means that the risk is generally well managed. One of the benefits of working on large buildings is that trades do not need to work on top of one another, with the risk of minor incidents accordingly reduced.

➔   Canary Wharf, including proposals by Richard
       Rogers Partnership (shown to right of the cluster),
       reflects the relative lack of constraints on either
       footprint or building form, resulting in large regular
       blocks which are relatively cost-effective to
       construct.
       Canary Wharf Group plc/© Miller Hare

Cost overview

Height is not the sole criterion in the consideration of the relative cost of tall buildings. The size of the floor plate, the overall proportion of the building, its location and degree of architectural expression will all have a fundamental impact on cost. This section looks at a number of indicative construction cost models based on building designs that vary according to these criteria.

Tall office buildings: for shell and core construction costs.

Principal cost drivers.
↓   © Davis Langdon LLP/KPF

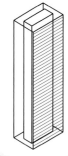

Site issues
Site constraints, such as adjoining structures and existing services obviously affect cost.

Height, shape and geometry
The most sensitive cost drivers are the specification and the extent of the frame and envelope. These are determined particularly by planning issues, the floor plate design and the environmental strategy, which affect the wall to floor ratio, structural complexity, core design and envelope performance criteria.

Life safety
Enhancements for safety and security, including requirements for bomb-blast measures to cladding, structural collapse resistance, fire protection enhancements, evacuation improvements and provision of diverse support systems are other drivers.

Services strategy
The environmental solution needs to be developed alongside the thermal performance of the façade. Cost drivers include: aesthetic intent, requirements for flexibility, building usage / operational issues, available space for plant and whole life costs.

Regulations and preferred practice
Design responses to Part L of the Building Regulations, together with enhanced performance for sustainability have cost implications.

Lift strategy
Population distribution, building functions, performance targets and factors that affect the core design, e.g. orientation of building entrances, structural considerations and escape strategies, all combine to influence the design and economics of the lifts and escalator installations.

Building ownership
Drivers include the quality of design and materials, investment to reduce whole life costs, applications for sustainability and requirements for flexibility and redundancy.

Building uses
The costs of single occupancy versus multi-let buildings and the design complexities associated with accommodating multiple uses within a single building are relevant.

Indicative costs

The following four models consider
indicative costs based on key design
variables relating to the design and
construction of tall buildings.

Floor to floor = 4m

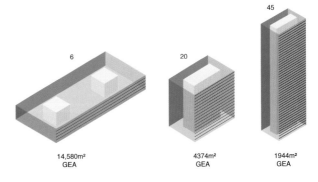

60

45

30

15

1944m²
GEA

1944m²
GEA

1944m²
GEA

1944m²
GEA

Cost Model One: Building height
Constant plan size, varying heights.
→   © Davis Langdon LLP/KPF

45   45   45   45

1215m²   1620m²   1944m²   2835m²
GEA   GEA   GEA   GEA

X 45 = 54,675m²   X 45 = 72,900m²   X 45 = 87,480m²   X 45 = 127,575m²

Cost Model Two: Plan size
Constant height, varying size floor plate.
→   © Davis Langdon LLP/KPF

Floor to floor = 4m

45

6   20

14,580m²   4374m²   1944m²
GEA   GEA   GEA

Cost Model Three: Proportion
Enclosing identical amounts of gross floor space in
buildings of varying height and floor plate.
→   © Davis Langdon LLP/KPF

Floor to floor = 4m

45   45

Urban periphery
Large floor plate, regular plan
Limited external articulation

2835m²   1944m²
GEA   GEA

City core
Small floor plate, irregular plan
Articulated, high performance envelope

Cost Model Four: Articulation
Comparing a more architecturally expressive building,
as could be required in the City of London, with the
'straight-up-and-down' form used for the base
analysis that is more feasible for a peripheral site.
→   © Davis Langdon LLP/KPF

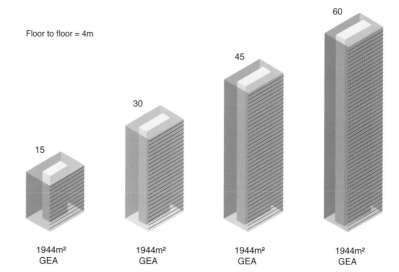

Floor to floor = 4m

15

30

45

60

1944m²
GEA

1944m²
GEA

1944m²
GEA

1944m²
GEA

→   Cost Model One: the impact of changing building
    height on building efficiency and cost.
    © Davis Langdon LLP/KPF

Cost Model One: height

Irrespective of floor plate, shape, form and other factors, tall buildings cost more to construct per unit of floor area than low rise buildings, despite the opportunities they offer in terms of repetition and sequencing. This relates to:

↘   their increased wind loadings and heavier frames

↘   their vertical transportation requirements, particularly lift capacities, speed, zoning, etc.

↘   the larger capacities of plant and distribution systems together with the increased pressures/hydraulic breaks that are required to deal with the increased vertical distances

↘   the effects of their scale and complexity on the movement of materials and labour

↘   the risks associated with their uniqueness and the fact that these risks are exacerbated by scale and the need to access a limited pool of skills and expertise

↘   the potential interest in including elective security and safety enhancements in response to possible risks (although acceptable responses can be provided at relatively little additional cost).

Cost Model One provides a notional indexing analysis for 15, 30, 45 and 60 storey buildings. It shows that the principal cost drivers that differentiate the taller from the shorter buildings (with constant floorplates) are: structure, façades and vertical transportation. In contrast to a typical city centre situation in which the building is likely to be more articulated (see Cost Model Four and associated discussion), this theoretical model is constructed with constant floor plates, thereby ensuring identical wall to floor ratios and hence relatively little difference in the cost of external walls. Arguably the most important finding that Cost Model One shows is the trend for floor area efficiencies to reduce as the constant floor plate building increases in height. The actual efficiency achieved will depend on various factors including: services strategy, structural design, lift arrangements and building use.

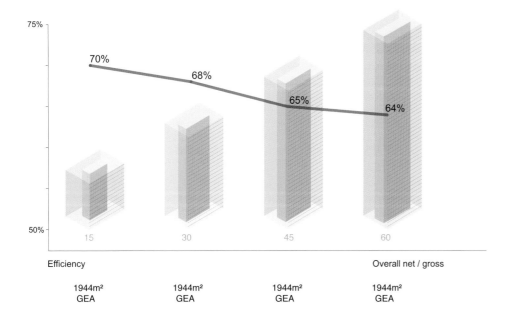

Efficiency

Overall net / gross

1944m²
GEA

1944m²
GEA

1944m²
GEA

1944m²
GEA

←   Efficiency: the ratio of net to
gross space – the building's
efficiency – will decline with
increased height. This reflects
the larger core area required to
serve a greater number of
floors.
© Davis Langdon LLP/KPF

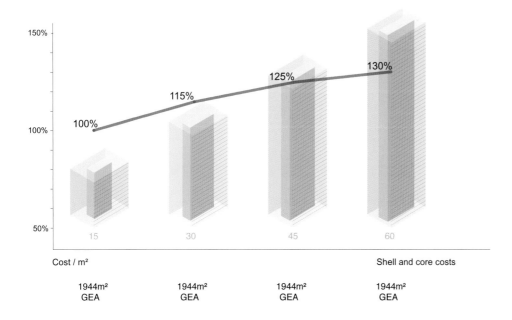

Cost / m²

Shell and core costs

1944m²
GEA

1944m²
GEA

1944m²
GEA

1944m²
GEA

←   Shell and core costs: shell and
core cost per m² rise with
buildings of increased height.
© Davis Langdon LLP/KPF

Main cost drivers of tall buildings

The relative effect of the four principal cost drivers will differ in each cost model.

Structure

The building's height, volumetric shape, plan form, core location and column spacings all combine to determine the most efficient and cost-effective structural solution. Irrespective of the structural system, the mass and cost of the structural frame will increase with height. Counteracting wind loads, which increase disproportionately with height, adds significantly to loads and costs.

Both material efficiency and buildability have a greater cost impact with height. These need to be considered hand-in-hand. An important factor will be the size of the structural members. This has a bearing on buildability and speed, and a possible impact on lettable floor areas. The selection of the structural system will therefore be determined by cost, building movement, space take-up, aesthetics, buildability and speed of construction. As with the other principal elements, it is important to focus on a single solution at an early stage of the design process.

Façades

Tall buildings are typically designed with a totally sealed external envelope. The façade's contribution to environmental control is crucial. With increasing attention to carbon emissions, the design of façades and services installations needs to be developed in unison.

More often than not, tall buildings will be all-glazed and the façades will comprise double walls (triple-glazed). It will be more efficient and sustainable to use the façade to control heat gain rather than rely on cooling installations to mitigate the performance of the envelope. A number of factors will affect how this is achieved. These are principally cost, performance, operational robustness, space take-up, aesthetics and ease of construction.

Beyond the detailed performance of the envelope, the design should seek to take maximum advantage of economies of scale, both in factory production and on site. With large areas of external walling (and high wall to floor ratios), efficiency of both production and installation are critical. This can be achieved by rationalising cladding types and fixing details through maximum repetition (without compromising aesthetics), ensuring that panels can be fixed from the floors rather than having to rely on cranes, and by unitising as much of the system as possible.

As well as the environmental strategy, the façade's interaction with the structural frame is important. Tolerances and movements should be addressed at the earliest opportunity, with slab edge live loads restricted to say 12-15mm to ensure a competitive curtain wall solution.

Should the design succeed in these respects, there is every reason to expect the economies of scale to offset any potential additional costs associated with factors such as increased wind loadings and logistics. However, the cost of the external walls is still likely to show a significant increase relative to those for low buildings, when expressed per unit of floor area, because of the higher wall to floor ratios that tend to be inherent to tall buildings. Slender tall buildings will be particularly affected in this respect.

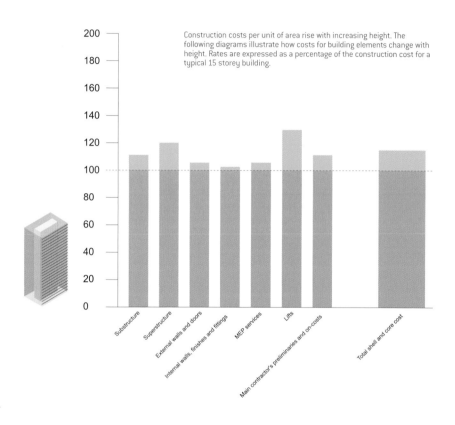

Construction costs per unit of area rise with increasing height. The following diagrams illustrate how costs for building elements change with height. Rates are expressed as a percentage of the construction cost for a typical 15 storey building.

↑   Elemental costs for a 30 storey building (baseline costs for a 15 storey building).
© Davis Langdon LLP/KPF

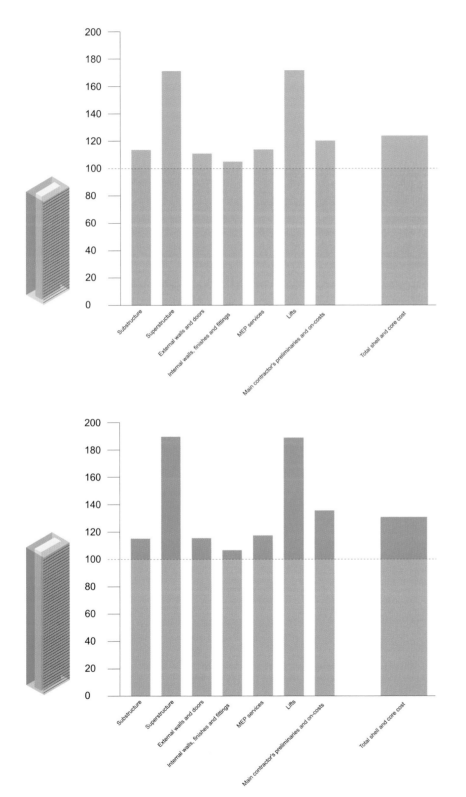

Vertical transportation

Core design is the crucial starting point for developing the internal operation of a tall building. It determines both the building's development efficiency and its operational effectiveness. Together with structural considerations, and to a lesser extent services distribution, the design of the lift installation is a fundamental part of optimising the core arrangement.

The aim of the lift and escalator installations is to optimise travel times and waiting intervals with the building's likely population profile in mind. Achieving this involves a significant level of specialist analysis, the result often representing a balance between number of lifts, lift speeds, size of groups, zoning of the building, core size and arrangement.

With an increase in building height comes an increase in strategic options to achieve these targets economically.

The fundamental options are:

⬊ Straightforward zoning of floors, with transfer levels

⬊ Sky lobbies served by express lifts

⬊ Double-deck lifts

⬊ A combination of the above.

The use of sophisticated controls, such as destination hall call, could be incorporated to improve overall performance. A cost/benefit analysis of such options will determine their attractiveness.

Main contractors' preliminaries/on-costs

Main contractors' preliminaries encompass a large complement of staff to manage the design and construction, and an array of accommodation, plant and equipment for use by the client, consultants, construction personnel and other site visitors. Care needs to be

taken to ensure the correct quality and scope of all these items to maximise efficiencies (and avoid unnecessary duplication with trade contractors' preliminaries).

Appropriate investment in main contractors' preliminaries will mitigate the pressures on trade contractors' preliminaries, which can often be considerably greater for a tall building project, partly due to the logistics of moving people and materials to and from the workface. The time taken by operatives travelling to and between floors and welfare facilities such as canteens and toilets can take up a significant part of the day.

It is important to minimise these inefficiencies and manage the construction process rigorously, starting with robust and detailed planning. An appropriate procurement strategy will also help to minimise programme and financial risks.

**Heron Tower, 110 Bishopsgate, KPF:
Construction sequence studies.**

↓ Demoltions: access and cranage.
    © KPF

↓ Basement construction: access and cranage.
    © KPF

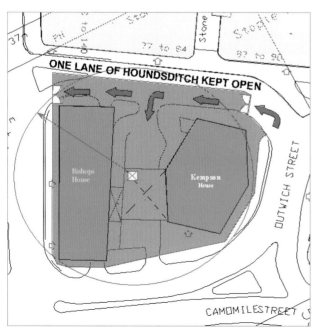

To achieve all this will require a significant level of input from a constructor, employed to manage the design team and the construction and site processes, and to provide an input into planning, procurement and cost control. This will include the provision, maintenance and co-ordination of common items of plant, facilities and equipment provided for use by all trade contractors. This level of input results in higher costs, associated with staff and plant equipment levels, which will need to be provided for relatively longer periods. The inherent cost and complexity of tall buildings will inevitably also result in relatively higher design and construction contingencies, when indexed against lower buildings (though percentage allowances will not necessarily be higher).

↓ Top down construction proposed for basements.
© KPF

↓ Superstructure construction: access and cranage.
© KPF

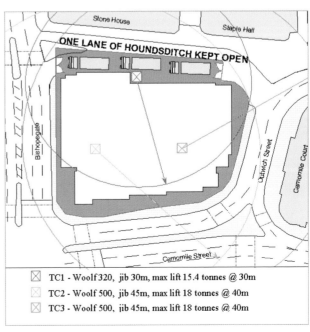

☒ TC1 - Woolf 320, jib 30m, max lift 15.4 tonnes @ 30m
☐ TC2 - Woolf 500, jib 45m, max lift 18 tonnes @ 40m
☒ TC3 - Woolf 500, jib 45m, max lift 18 tonnes @ 40m

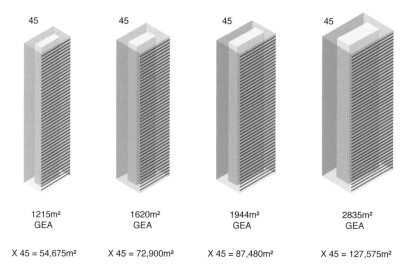

| 45 | 45 | 45 | 45 |

| 1215m²
GEA | 1620m²
GEA | 1944m²
GEA | 2835m²
GEA |

→ Cost Model Two:
impact of size of the floor plate on the efficiency
and cost of a 45 storey tower.
© Davis Langdon LLP/KPF

| X 45 = 54,675m² | X 45 = 72,900m² | X 45 = 87,480m² | X 45 = 127,575m² |

Cost Model Two: plan size

The 45 storey building from the earlier analysis has been further reviewed to consider the effect of alternative floor plate sizes – 1,215m², 1,620m² and 2,835m² – on area and cost (re-indexed to the tall building).

The effect of varying floor plates on the shell and core cost of a tall building shows the principal cost drivers to be:

↘ Wall-to-floor ratios
The significantly higher wall-to-floor ratio of a smaller floor plate will result in a greater proportion of costs being attributed to the envelope. It will also affect the services strategy, which will have to respond to an increased level of solar gain.

↘ Structure
Slender tall buildings require stronger frame solutions for increased stiffness, to counteract the more marked effects of wind action.

↘ Lifts
A higher lift density will be required to serve the needs of smaller 'premium' occupiers.

Additionally, where the floor plate is significantly reduced in slender tall buildings, opportunities for economies of scale may be reduced or lost. Net to gross floor area efficiences are also shown to deteriorate with a decrease in the size of the floor plate, relating to relatively larger cores on smaller floor plates.

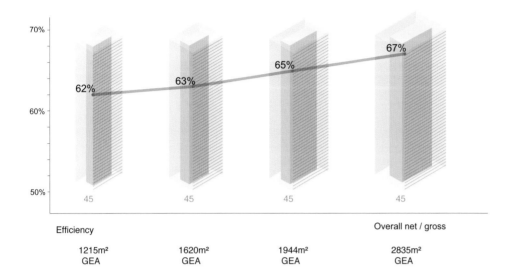

Efficiency

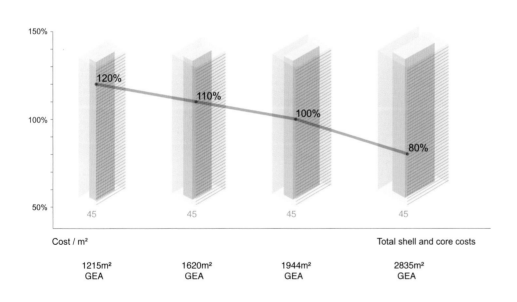

Cost / m²

Cost Model Three: proportion

Cost Model Three considers the choice of building form for a given amount of gross floor area. It shows three possibilities to provide around 87,000m² of total gross internal floor area: a groundscraper of 6 storeys (14,580m² floor plate), a medium-rise building of 20 storeys (4,374m² floor plate), and the 45 storey office building which was analysed previously. This comparison results in the following indicative effect upon the total cost indices.

The combination of decreasing height and increasing floor plate affords:

↘ Significantly improved wall-to-floor ratios

↘ More efficiently designed elements (such as the structural frame)

↘ Faster construction, with a greater proportion of the building being horizontal rather than vertical, and easier logistics

↘ More options in the location of components such as central plant.

Floor to floor = 4m

→ Cost Model Three:
impact of proportion on
building cost.
© Davis Langdon LLP/KPF

6	20	45	
14,580m² GEA	4374m² GEA	1944m² GEA	

→ Efficiency
© Davis Langdon LLP/KPF

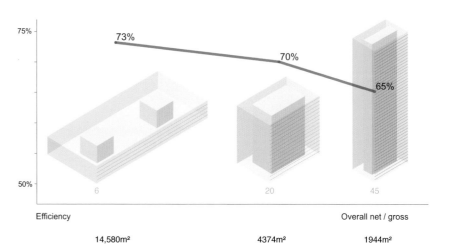

Efficiency   Overall net / gross

14,580m²   4374m²   1944m²
GEA   GEA   GEA

Cost Model Four: articulation

This compares a predominantly functional, well detailed but essentially plain building form, such as HSBC at Canary Wharf, with a more complex, articulated building typical of the City of London. The comparison illustrates key implications of designing and procuring a tall building in a sensitive city centre location. These include:

⬃ Complex substructures to avoid existing obstructions and deal with boundary conditions

⬃ A more complicated shape and form, particularly in response to planning considerations (e.g. the tapered shape of the proposal for 122 Leadenhall Street, predominantly to avoid a viewing corridor to St Paul's Cathedral)

⬃ The higher quality of design and materials

⬃ The increased pressures to incorporate an attractive interaction between the building and the streetscape, an architectural statement at its pinnacle, and more demanding planning requirements

⬃ More complex construction issues resulting in extended construction programmes.

By far the biggest impact on costs will be the more complex building form, a simplified illustration of which is shown in Cost Model Four (noting that real examples of this exist, e.g. the Heron, Minerva and London Bridge Towers).

Floor area efficiencies are also likely to be reduced, possibly through a less straightforward core design and more impact of structure on the floor plate.

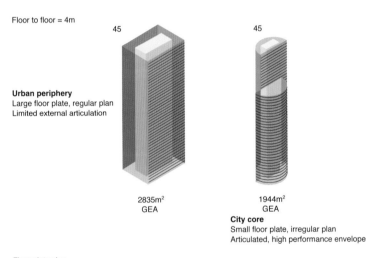

Floor to floor = 4m

Urban periphery
Large floor plate, regular plan
Limited external articulation

2835m² GEA

1944m² GEA

City core
Small floor plate, irregular plan
Articulated, high performance envelope

Floor plate size

← Cost Model Four: articulation
© Davis Langdon LLP/KPF

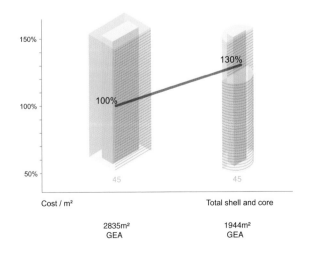

Cost / m²   Total shell and core

2835m² GEA   1944m² GEA

← Shell and core costs
© Davis Langdon LLP/KPF

Cost and height

The following principles are involved:

⭆ For a constant floor plate, costs per m² of floor area increase with height, whilst overall net to gross floor area efficiencies are reduced.

⭆ The cost/height relationship is characterised by step changes, due to various technical thresholds which occur at different heights and floor plate dimensions. The full cost progression depends on the specific aggregation of the component costs in any given design.

⭆ Larger floor plates are more economic, mainly due to their superior net to gross floor area efficiencies and improved wall to floor ratios.

⭆ City schemes constructed in high value locations involve a trade-off, with reduced floor area efficiencies and higher cost, because of their more articulated façades, more complex forms and the other implications of a constrained, sensitive location.

⭆ Groundscrapers can provide more net area for the same overall gross area provision, at significantly lower construction costs, but involve less intense – and potentially less sustainable – use of high value land.

Risk

Cost-effective enhancements can promote safety in tall buildings, addressing evacuation, structural collapse and bomb-blast resistance. With building management and occupant training, these measures offer economically viable inputs to risk assessment.

A question of value

With many factors at play, the cost indices provided here are necessarily indicative.

Because of the increased unit costs and decrease in floor area efficiency with taller buildings, net space is disproportionately more expensive. The viability graph (opposite) illustrates this by plotting the cost in accordance with net internal floor area.

Irrespective of floor plates, landmark status, form and proportion, development costs per m² of gross floor area increase with height. To be viable, the value of tall buildings per m² must also be higher, and market evidence suggests that it is possible for tall buildings to provide an acceptable long-term return.

The economics of tall buildings on both a macro and micro scale will vary according to their location. The values and costs associated with a tall building in the Far East are different to one in London. London is a 'young market' for tall buildings. With the increased knowledge and experience that comes as more proposals are developed, the cost and efficiency premiums may be reduced. The distinctiveness of quality tall buildings may also represent a valuable form of diversification within the office sector.

Tall buildings:
The pressures on a potential viability curve

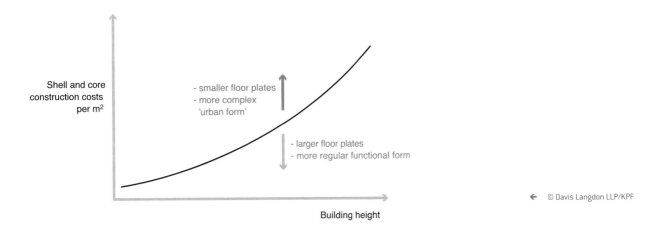

© Davis Langdon LLP/KPF

↘ Irrespective of floor plates, landmark status, form and proportion, development costs per m^2 of gross floor area increase with height. To be viable, the value of tall buildings per m^2 must also be higher, and market evidence suggests that it is possible for tall buildings to provide an acceptable long-term return.

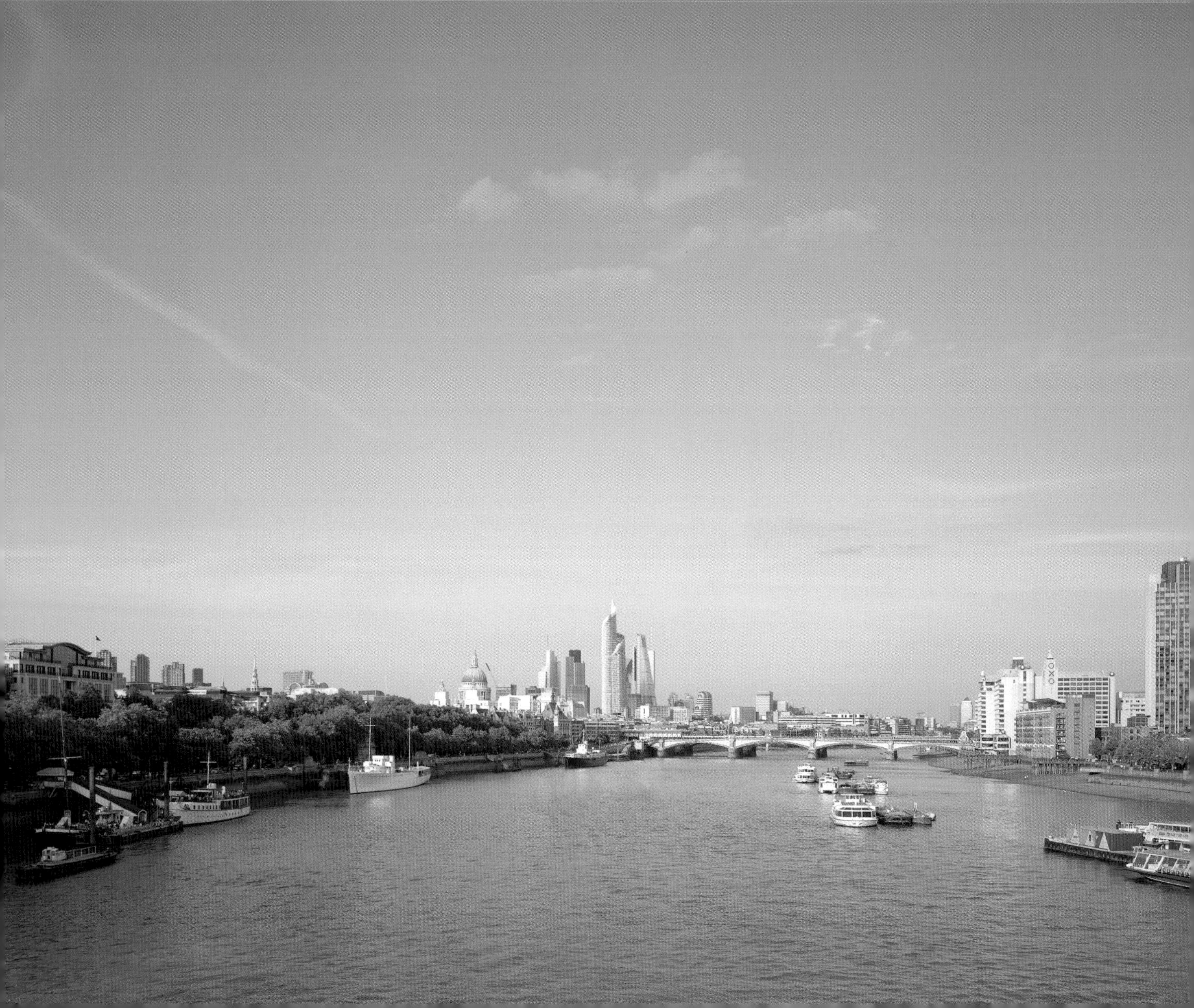

the sustainability agenda:

↘ Tall buildings can promote sustainable development and living patterns. Sited close to the concentration of public transport nodes in urban centres, their relatively higher densities facilitate intensive use of urban land, limiting development of greenfield sites. Located thus, they can avoid the high impact of dispersed travel by private car. Given that such travel currently accounts for most of the 25% of carbon dioxide emissions generated by transport overall, this is relevant. Where tall buildings incorporate a mix of uses in individual buildings or in urban clusters, they can further support a reduction in travel to meet a range of living needs.

ZIONA STRELITZ ZZA

Energy in use

Appropriately oriented and integrally designed with holistic building servicing systems, the energy used by new tall buildings can be reduced relative to the demands of earlier tall buildings. The distinctly energy intensive aspects of tall buildings are vertical travel and the ratio of external surface to enclosed area. Recent proposals for tall buildings demonstrate scope to target energy efficient design in combination with user comfort. The key to this is integrated design, with respect to building location, orientation, façade treatment and the systems for key building services. Innovations in passive control and high performance façades are especially promising.

Payback on capital investment

Whilst tall buildings are more costly to construct, the large enclosed area they provide relative to their frequently high value site area can match or exceed the additional capital investment required at project outset. Some return may also derive from a rental premium associated with an enhanced operating environment, especially if this is associated with environmentally friendly internal space, accommodation that suits a range of functions, and scope for energy transfer between complementary building uses.

← Prospective Thameside panorama
© Hayes Davidson/KPF

about the contributors:

HARRY BRIDGES is a director and structural engineer in Arup, with widely based experience technically and geographically. He has collaborated on tall buildings in London, Europe and Asia, and on transport projects, deep basements, and high capacity foundations.

ADRIAN GODWIN, a chartered engineer, is Chairman of Lerch, Bates & Associates, Europe. The holder of several patents, and with expertise in the development of smart elevator control systems and planning elevator systems for tall buildings, he has been involved in the design of the lift systems for some of the tallest buildings in Europe and the Middle East.

FRED PILBROW, architect, is a director at KPF's London office where he has been responsible for designing significant projects, including the Rothermere American Institute at the University of Oxford, the restoration of Princes Gardens for Imperial College and the Cyprus House for Representatives in Nicosia. Tall buildings are a particular focus of his work. He has been responsible for some of KPF's notable tall building designs including New London Bridge House, HQ1 Canary Wharf and the Heron Tower.

ZIONA STRELITZ, social anthropologist, town planner and interior designer, founded and directs ZZA Research and Consulting. ZZA focuses on locational, spatial, social, cultural and management issues, to promote effective use of built settings, specialising in user research, briefing and evaluation. She led the consultation with Londoners for LPAC's Strategic Review of Planning Guidance for Tall Buildings, and the BCO's research, *Giving Occupiers a Voice*.

FAITH WAINWRIGHT, structural engineer, is a director of Arup and fellow of the Royal Academy of Engineering. She was a member of Arup's Extreme Events Mitigation Task force convened immediately after the events of 11 September 2001, and on the committee of the Institution of Structural Engineer's working party on Safety in Tall Buildings.

STEVE WATTS, quantity surveyor, is a Partner at Davis Langdon LLP, heading their Tall Buildings Specialist Group. He led their team on the HSBC tower at Canary Wharf from inception to completion, and has worked on a number of tall buildings schemes, including 122 Leadenhall Street and London Bridge Tower.

MOHSEN ZIKRI, chartered engineer, is a Director of Arup with an interest in sustainability of tall buildings. He delivers projects that combine exciting architecture with innovating building services solutions. He works with key clients and leading architects on notable projects.

acknowledgements:

We wish to thank the following individuals and organisations for their generosity in arranging and/or granting permission for the use of images in this publication.

Alsop & Partners
Arcaid – Richard Bryant
Arup
Ateliers, Jean Nouvel
Barclays
Canary Wharf Group plc
CentralPhotography.com
CityScape
Clifford Chance
David Hawkins
David J Osborn
Davis Langdon LLP
Eamonn O'Mahony
Foreman Roberts
Foster and Partners
Frederic Terreaux
GMJ
Grimshaw
H.G. Esch
Hayes Davidson
Ian Lambot
Ian Simpson Architects
John Mclean
Justin Piperger
Katsuisha Kida (RRP)
Kenny IP
KPF

Lerch Bates Associates
Melon Studio
Miller Hare
Nigel Young (Foster and Partners)
Pringle Brandon
Renzo Piano Building Workshop
Richard Davies
Richard Rogers Partnership
Richard Seifert and Partners
Skidmore, Owings & Merrill LLP
Smoothe Ltd
STP Photography
Timothy Hursley
www.foliophotography.co.uk
www.uniform.net
ZZA

If anyone has been left off this list, this is entirely inadvertent and we apologise and thank them too.

Thanks to Robert Peebles and Ian Walker of KPF for their input to the section on 'The Envelope'. Thanks to Joanne Aufrichtig and Victoria Scalongne for their help with production at ZZA.

A special thank you to Clare Mason of KPF for extensive support in the production of this book.

index:

The British Council for Offices (BCO)

The British Council for Offices (BCO) exists to research, develop and communicate best practice in all aspects of the office sector. It delivers this by providing a forum for the discussion and debate of relevant issues.

The BCO works to promote co-operation and understanding between landlord and tenant, investor and developer and owner and occupier, thereby improving efficiency and innovation in the sector.

Further information about the BCO, including the membership application form, can be found on the BCO website www.bco.org.uk or please contact us at:

38 Lombard Street
London
EC3V 9BS

Tel: 020 7283 4588
Fax: 020 7626 2223
Email: mail@bco.org.uk